The Economics of Affirmative Action

The Economics of Affirmative Action

James V. Koch
Illinois State University

John F. Chizmar, Jr.
Illinois State University

Lexington Books

D.C. Heath and Company
Lexington, Massachusetts
Toronto   London

Library of Congress Cataloging in Publication Data

Chizmar, John F
    The economics of affirmative action.

    Bibliography: p. 149
    Includes index.
    1. Illinois. State University, Normal—Personnel management. 2. Affirmative action programs—Illinois—Normal. 3. Discrimination in employment—Illinois—Normal. 4. Sex discrimination against women—Illinois—Normal. I. Koch, James V., joint author. II. Title.
LD2347.C44   658.3'044   75-32872
ISBN 0-669-00362-X

Published simultaneously in Canada.

Printed in the United States of America.

International Standard Book Number: 0-669-00362-X

Library of Congress Catalog Card Number: 75-32872

To Chris, Joelle, Donna, Beth, and Mark

Contents

List of Figures

List of Figures

List of Tables

Acknowledgments

The authors owe great thanks to President Gene Budig and Provost James Horner of Illinois State University for their encouragement and understanding of this study. The data requirements of this study have been immense. Dr. Warren Harden, Director of Institutional Research at Illinois State University, was patient and generous in his assistance in this area. Dr. Dorothy Carrington, Affirmative Action Officer for Women at Illinois State University, provided the authors with several different types of assistance. The authors benefited from the comments of the dean of the College of Arts and Sciences, Barbara Uehling, as well as those of Professors L. Dean Hiebert and David Spencer. The manuscript was typed in superb fashion by Cherry Slaton.

This study does *not* reflect an official institutional position or viewpoint on the part of Illinois State University. Similarly, the conclusions drawn by the authors may or may not be indicative of the opinions of the individuals noted above. The defects of the study, as well as the opinions expressed, must be attributed solely to the authors.

The Economics of Affirmative Action

1 Introduction

> The Constitution of these United States says that all *men* are created equal.
> It don't say nothing about women.
>
> *Anonymous*

Sex discrimination against women in employment is a widespread and pernicious problem.[1] At the same time, however, there is widespread agreement in nearly all respectable quarters that sex discrimination against women in employment is undesirable from an ethical standpoint. A host of federal and state laws now exist which seek to eliminate the practice and the case against sex discrimination against women in the area of employment. Further, the case against sex discrimination against women in employment is strengthened by economic theory and empirical evidence, both of which suggest that considerable productivity losses occur because of discriminatory use and reward of women employees. In a word, discrimination against women employees is usually uneconomic.[2]

Despite the consensus noted above, affirmative action programs designed to eliminate the practice and effects of sex discrimination against women in employment have often provoked opposition and controversy. This is not a case of women employees vis-a-vis men employees. Sexist notions and practices are seldom overcome in a few years, or even in a generation.

Nevertheless, it is disturbing that individuals of presumably goodwill who oppose sex discrimination in employment have hypothesized that affirmative action programs may induce inefficient behavior on the part of employers with respect to the evaluations and reward of employees, as well as with respect to the employment decision itself. Richard Lester, for example, has drawn upon his experiences as a dean at Princeton University in asserting that affirmative action programs may cause a decline in faculty quality and performance.[3] At the same time, however, this charge has been challenged strongly by others who argue that there is no reliable empirical evidence which supports such a conclusion.[4]

Whatever the import of the empirical evidence, or lack thereof, concerning the effects of affirmative action programs, it is fair to say that the number of firms and universities that currently have affirmative action programs, and which claim to be "equal opportunity, affirmative action" employers, is not only large, but growing. Presidential Executive Order 11,246 (1965) requires nearly all federal contractors, including universities that receive federal monies for research or other purposes, to sign an agreement to not discriminate against any employee

1

on the basis of race, color, religion, or national origin. Presidential Executive
Order 11,375, which took effect in October 1968, extended this coverage to
include discrimination on the basis of sex. Both executive orders require contractors to file a written affirmative action agreement describing that contractor's program to eliminate past or present inequities. The so-called Philadelphia Plan, which imposed specific hiring quotas upon Philadelphia-area trade
unions, is a prime example of a negotiated affirmative action plan that resulted
from the executive orders. Failure to comply brings with it the denial of lucrative federal contracts and potential court suits. Hence, nearly any employer
of importance today has an affirmative action plan to eliminate past or present
inequities in employment or compensation. The Philadelphia Plan, which imposed specific minority employee hiring quotas, is an example of an affirmative
action plan that was hammered out in sometimes bitter negotiations between
various agencies of the federal government and the Philadelphia trade unions.
This agreement will be examined in greater detail later because of its landmark
status.

Failure of an employer to comply with the law or executive orders concerning affirmative action can result in court suits and/or the denial to the
employer of lucrative federal contracts. In the case of universities, the scope
of contract denial extends far beyond contracts for hard research; it includes
scholarship and financial aid assistance to students, building and equipment
subsidies, and even driver education funding. Hence, even the threat of denial
of such funds is a potent weapon. In June 1975, the Department of Health,
Education, and Welfare warned 29 colleges and universities that they might lose
a total of $65 million in federal contracts because of affirmative action defi-
ciencies.[5] As a consequence, rare is the employer of any importance who does
not have a written affirmative action plan which supposedly translates into action.

The Lack of Empirical Evidence

Whereas there is ample evidence detailing the existence of sex discrimination
against women in employment, there is almost no evidence concerning the actual
effects of affirmative action programs. There are several reasons for this deficiency. First, when a given employer has been guilty of sex discrimination against
women employees, that employer is ordinarily loath to publicize that fact. Sex
discrimination is frowned upon even in a male-dominated society. Hence, even
when employers feel they are not guilty of sex discrimination charges, they will
soft-pedal the fact that they have agreed to, or been forced to adopt, an affirmative action program designed to erase the practice and effects of sex discrimination.

Any meaningful statement about the operation of an affirmative action program must be couched in terms of salaries, promotions, penalties, and so forth. In particular, wage and salary information is ordinarily considered to be confidential in nature. Employee Jones is ordinarily not entitled to know what employee Smith's salary and productivity are or have been. This has usually meant that data concerning the operation of affirmative action programs have been highly aggregative in nature. For example, the University of California at Berkeley agreed early in 1975 to hire an additional 100 minority faculty members over the next 30 years.[6] Similarly, American Telephone and Telegraph Company admitted to agreeing to pay over $2.5 million to correct widespread deficiencies in the way it has carried out a landmark equal employment settlement with the federal government.[7] The revised settlement called for payments of $125 to $1,500 to as many as 2,500 qualified people whose promotions may have been unnecessarily delayed, according to *Women Today*.[8] The relevant point is that such information makes it impossible to judge anything except the intention of the University of California at Berkeley to hire more minority faculty, and the intention of American Telephone and Telegraph Company to pay penalty wages to a large group of employees. It is impossible to judge whether such settlements were adequate in size, or even whether any such settlements were merited. Further, there is absolutely no hint whether the settlements deal effectively with the circumstances of individual employees or faculty. We do not know, and have no way to determine, if the practice and effects of discrimination against employee Brown have increased, decreased, or remained the same as a result of the agreements. Aggregation, then, is a second reason why we know so little about the economic effects of affirmative action programs.

An important goal of affirmative action programs is the attainment of "equal pay for equal work." Employees should be paid on the basis of their objective performance on the job rather than on the basis of some extraneous factor such as sex or race. There is no legal requirement that men and women be paid the same. Instead, the legal requirement is that men and women employees be paid impartially according to the same criteria. Hence, employees with differing performance characteristics will be paid differing salaries, have differing promotional patterns, and perhaps even differing probabilities of being hired for a given job in the first place. Unfortunately, measures of the productivity of individual employees, and supervisor or peer group evaluations of a particular employee's performance, are generally unavailable. This has rendered impossible the determination of whether "equal pay for equal work" has been achieved by a particular affirmative action program in a particular set of cases. Once again, published data tell us that an affirmative action program is being conducted. Such data do not lead to even tentative conclusions about the success of that program. It does not suffice to report that the mean salary of women employees is less than/equal to/greater than the mean salary of men employees before and after affirmative action. Salary means are irrelevant unless controlled for employee performance and productivity, as well as other characteristics. The paucity of such data has seriously reduced the number of empirical studies that have made meaningful empirical statements about the economic effects of affirmative action programs.

The Boundaries of This Study

This study examines the economic effects of the operation of an affirmative action salary-increment program for women faculty at Illinois State University. It does not deal with affirmative action efforts undertaken in behalf of minority or black faculty members; however, such faculty are clearly included in the coverage of the law and regulations concerning affirmative action, and were also dispensed special salary increments as a part of a general affirmative action program at Illinois State University.

The center of attention in this study is the compensation and reward of over 530 full-time nonadministrative, permanent faculty at Illinois State University. Two basic questions are addressed in the study. First, was an affirmative action salary program for women faculty required at the University? Second, what were the economic implications of the affirmative action program that was actually undertaken?

The availability of data has dictated the limitation of the empirical evidence presented in this study to academia, and more specifically to Illinois State University. This limitation enables the authors to present empirical evidence which, for example, takes into account the differential productivity of faculty members. This is crucial if a legitimate determination is to be made on the "equal pay for equal work" issue. Similarly, the data set includes detailed information concerning the academic rank, training, age, and so forth, of each faculty member. Once again, determination of whether sex discrimination against women faculty exists in salaries and whether there is, in fact, equal pay for equal work depends upon such factors. Such microeconomic detailed data are simply not available elsewhere. It is for this reason that the empirical evidence in this study relates to a particular academic institution. The authors recognize that the evidence presented may have limited applicability in certain other situations where the measurements of employment, evaluation, and productivity differ greatly. At the same time, the basic aims of affirmative action salary programs are the same both inside and outside academia. The lessons drawn here, and the discussion of the problems encountered, should be of great utility to all individuals and employers connected with affirmative action programs, whatever their genesis and operation. The methodology and approach of this study can be generalized and applied to other situations with relative ease.

Other studies of affirmative action programs have highlighted the hiring process. For example, the aforementioned affirmative action program at the University of California at Berkeley concentrates on the future hiring of women and minority faculty rather than on the short-run problem of eliminating wage discrimination against these same faculty classes. This study is not concerned with the hiring aspects of affirmative action programs. There are several reasons for this choice. The motivating factor, however, is the relative lack of reliable data concerning the hiring process at any university or firm. Most employers have exceedingly poor records concerning applicants for the jobs they advertise. Further, it is difficult to ascertain who is actually in the potential pool of individuals that can be hired. For example, should the pool of potential employees include individuals who are foreign-born and of foreign citizenship, but who receive their academic degrees in the United States? If so, then the pool will contain far more minority faculty than otherwise. The primary problem, however, is that hiring is often done on the basis of either an interview or the quality of a presentation made by the prospective employee. The quality of the employee in such a circumstance is largely unknown. In sum, it is extremely difficult to devise a methodology which would result in a meaningful test of affirmative action in the area of employment. This study does not attempt to do so.

This is not a conventional study of sex discrimination, although the foundation of any evaluation of the economic effects of an affirmative action salary program must be strongly based upon the evidence relating to the existence and location of any sex discrimination that might exist in the salary structure. Indeed, the demonstration that salary sex discrimination has occurred, or is occurring, is a necessary rationale for the implementation of an affirmative action salary program. On this score, there is strong evidence, some of which has been contributed by the authors, that there is pervasive discrimination against women faculty in salaries.[9] The *need* for affirmative action salary programs has been established in a wide range of situations. What has been lacking is a monitoring process by which the economic effects of the affirmative action program are observed and the success of the affirmative action program is evaluated. That is the concern of this study. The authors not only suggest a general methodology by which the need for affirmative action salary programs can be evaluated, but also apply this methodology in the case of over 100 women faculty members who received affirmative action salary increments at Illinois State University. The economic effects of this program, particularly in terms of resource allocation, are observed and appraised.

Finally, this is not a study of the process by which academic ranks are earned or assigned. At the same time, it is true that the rank of academic faculty member is often related to the salary of that faculty member. For that reason, sex discrimination in the granting of faculty rank will sometimes spill over into the salary structure. At Illinois State University, however, no salary schedule exists for faculty which connects academic rank to dollars. Also, no monetary raise is tied to the promotion of a faculty member to a higher academic rank. Hence, the process by which rank is attained is of secondary importance here. The authors have, however, investigated the determinants of academic rank at Illinois State University and will cite the results of that work later where it is relevant to salary determination.

The Position and Approach of the Authors

Sex discrimination and affirmative action programs are controversial subjects which seem to attract passionate defenses and/or attacks even more rapidly than the appearance of new federal grant programs garner proposals to spend the newly authorized money. The motives of anyone who undertakes a study in the areas of sex discrimination and affirmative action are often openly challenged and frequently considered suspect. The authors accept this situation as a fact of life and are reconciled to receiving both emotional and factual criticisms regardless of the findings reported here. Indeed, the empirical evidence presented in this study will probably produce anger both among strong feminists and among male chauvinists.

The authors subscribe to the viewpoint that there is a distinction between *positive* and *normative* economics.[10] Positive economics deals with "what is," and is independent of any particular moral or ethical premises. Normative economics deals with "what ought to be" or "what should be," and is that area of economic analysis where value judgments and moral-ethical preferences are invited. *The Economics of Affirmative Action* is in the tradition of positive economics.

The interest of this study is in determining how affirmative action salary programs actually operate, and what their actual economic effects are. The impact of the affirmative action program upon resource allocation and an evaluation of the program in terms of economic efficiency are also matters of positive economics and are considered in this book. These types of questions can be answered independent of whether the authors (or the readers) approve or disapprove of equal pay for equal work, or are radical feminists, male chauvinist pigs, somewhere in between, or totally disinterested.

The acceptance of a distinction between positive economics and normative economics does not prevent either economists or lay people from adopting or preaching a particular normative point of view. Citizen and economist alike are free to adopt any value premises that they wish. Those values, however, should not interfere with the determination of "what is." Once a determination of "what is" has been made, then the economist can make normative judgments concerning "what ought to be." Note, however, that economists have no special competence in the areas of ethics and morals. The tools of the economist do not yield conclusions about what is just or equitable in the area of affirmative action or in any other arena.

It is the value judgment of the authors that sex discrimination is a reprehensible and immoral practice. Similarly, the authors are inclined to disapprove of any salary or compensation procedure which rewards employees on a basis other than the productivity and performance of those employees. The authors would prefer a "meritocracy" where individuals prosper or fail badly on the basis of their demonstrated merit and productivity. Further, the authors favor programs designed to eliminate the practice and effects of sex discrimination in employment. Affirmative action salary programs are one example of this type of program.

Despite the authors' confessed bias against sex discrimination and in favor of programs designed to eliminate the practice and effects of sex discrimination, it does not follow that the authors automatically approve of all affirmative action salary programs. Nor does it follow that the authors' judgment about what is moral in this area should color their empirical analysis of the affirmative action salary program at Illinois State University. This is consistent with both the spirit and the letter of the positive economic philosophy.

The Plan of This Study

The legal basis for affirmative action programs is contained in general form in the Constitution of the United States, particularly in the Preamble and the Fourteenth Amendment. The actual operational basis, however, is several presidential executive orders and other interpretive regulations issued by federal agencies. These orders and regulations are overlapping and sometimes conflicting. Enforcement duties have been allocated to over a dozen different agencies. Chapter 2 deals with this morass and attempts to sketch current policy in light of historical developments.

The justification for affirmative action programs is the existence of sex discrimination. Several competing theories explain why sex discrimination occurs and the conditions under which it is likely to appear. These models, including the Marxian variant, are analyzed in Chapter 3, and the theoretical predictions of the models are highlighted so that they can be examined later in light of the empirical evidence presented.

The number of empirical studies relating to sex discrimination is almost legion. However, only a few of these have been methodologically sound. These studies are reviewed and critiqued in Chapter 4, and note is made of untested hypotheses that remain. Empirical studies of the economics of affirmative action programs are very few in number. These studies, and their limitations, are also examined in Chapter 4.

The theoretical model that underpins the empirical work in this study and the actual empirical work are presented in Chapter 5. Particular emphasis is placed upon the factual-counterfactual methodology that is the keystone of this study. Emphasis is placed upon the relationship of the factual-counterfactual methodology to the legal requirements for affirmative action, and especially to the equal-pay-for-equal-work criterion.

The implications of the empirical work for economic efficiency and resource allocation are examined in Chapter 6. Further, the success of the affirmative action salary program in meeting its goals is examined. The policy and equity aspects of the empirical evidence are analyzed. The generality of both the methodology and the empirical evidence is also considered here.

2 The Legal Setting

... by and large the performance of Amèrican judges in the area of sex discrimination can be succinctly described as ranging from poor to abominable.

The idea that men and women stand as equals in the face of the law is a relatively new development. The founding fathers did not regard as debatable the premise that women were to restrict their activities to home and hearth. The traditional German prescription for women, "Kinder, Kuchen, Kirche," that is, "children, cake, church," was widely regarded as the correct model. Women were neither expected nor allowed to participate in most political and economic decisions. As Thomas Jefferson noted, "Were our state a pure democracy, there would still be excluded from our deliberations women, who, to prevent deprivations of morals and ambiguity of issues, should not mix promiscuously in gatherings of men."[1]

Despite the efforts of such early feminists as Abigail Adams and others,[2] the Constitution, as it took effect in 1788, was mute on the role and rights of women as citizens. Women were citizens; however, they were not expected, nor generally allowed, to vote. The Preamble spoke of "We the People of the United States," and women were included in the population census for purposes of determining congressional representation. At the same time, when the Constitution referred to the President of the United States, the pronoun "he" was used. The Bill of Rights, ratified in 1791, offers an interesting view of the attitudes of the times. It cited the rights of "citizens" and "persons," and extended those rights to *all* such citizens or persons. At the same, pronouns such as "himself" crept into several of the amendments comprising the Bill of Rights.

Hence, there was no language in the Constitution which directly prohibited women from voting, serving in the Congress, or being elected to various federal offices. Nonetheless, this was both the understanding and the practice at the time. Such an interpretation was consistent with the Declaration of Independence, which had earlier declared that "all Men are created equal," and had notably ignored the plight and existence of women. As Alexis de Tocqueville dispassionately noted in his famous *Democracy in America,* "In no country has

---

John D. Johnston and Charles L. Knapp, "Sex Discrimination by Law: A Study in Judicial Perspective," *New York University Law Review,* 46 (October 1971), p. 676.

such constant care been taken as in America to trace two clearly distinct lines of action for the two sexes. . . . American women never manage the outward concerns of the family, or conduct a business, or take part in political life."[3]

In the nineteenth century and first half of the twentieth century, the force of custom and long-ingrained attitudes was often more important than law in constraining the legal rights and activities of women. Consider the following editorial statement by the *New York Herald,* Horace Greeley's newspaper, in 1852:

> How did woman first become subject to man as she is now all over the world? By her nature, her sex, just as the negro, is and always will be, to the end of time, inferior to the white race, and, therefore doomed to subjection; but happier than she would be in any other condition, just because it is the law of her nature. The women themselves would not have the law reversed.[4]

It was not until the Nineteenth Amendment was ratified in 1920 that the right of suffrage was guaranteed for women. The extension of suffrage to women, however, did not have any immediate effect upon the myriad of laws, regulations, and attitudes upon which the foundation of sex discrimination against women was built. The performance of the judiciary in this area was glacially slow. Until 1971, the United States Supreme Court never rejected any sex line which had been written into law. Finally, in *Reed* v. *Reed* (1971) the Court invalidated a South Carolina statute on the basis that it required unacceptable sex discrimination against women.[5] The judiciary trailed the development of public opinion in the area of sex discrimination and refused to rule upon many issues which involved practices that were, by today's standards, blatantly sexist in character.

The Constitution of the United States

There is little doubt that the original Constitution was written with the intent of excluding women from voting and most public offices. At the same time, there are no specific statements in the Constitution which place limitations on the rights or citizenship of women. Indeed, the Fourteenth Amendment (1868) promises "equal protection of the law" to "all persons born or naturalized in the United States."[6] The Fourteenth Amendment forbids states from making or enforcing any law which would ". . . abridge the privileges or immunities of citizens of the United States. . . ."[7] These statements would seem to be rather strong, obvious constitutional prohibitions against sex discrimination, and they have served as the basis for considerable legislation and action in the last fifteen years. Women are denied the equal protection of the

law when they are subjected to discrimination which, if directed at men, would
be illegal. In the context of 1868, however, the Fourteenth Amendment was
designed to apply to male blacks, many of whom had been slaves until the Civil
War.

While the Fourteenth Amendment would appear to prevent sex discrimination from being written into law, it was traditionally not given that interpretation by the courts. Women were generally denied the right to vote until the
Nineteenth Amendment (1920) took effect. Further, as outlined above, it was
not until 1971 that the Supreme Court finally invalidated a state statute which
resulted in sex discrimination. By 1971, however, many supplementary laws
concerning sex discrimination had been passed, and several presidential executive orders had been promulgated, which visibly strengthened (forced) the hand
of the Court on this matter. It is fair to assert that the Fourteenth Amendment
has not played a significant part in sex discrimination cases despite its apparent
applicability.

Equal Pay Act (1963)

The Equal Pay Act represents the first important operational piece of federal
legislation designed to eliminate sex discrimination in employment and compensation. The act states that "No employer . . . shall discriminate . . . between employees on the basis of sex by paying wages to employees . . . at a rate less than
the rate at which he pays wages to employees of the opposite sex . . . for equal
work on jobs the performance of which requires equal skill, effort, and responsibility, and which are performed under similar working conditions. . . ."[8] Three
basic exceptions to this wide dictum are permitted. Differences in compensation
for men and women on similar jobs are permitted if the differences result from:
(1) a seniority system, (2) a merit system, or (3) a system which measures earnings by quantity or quality of production.

The Equal Pay Act is the primary basis for one of the oft-stated goals of
affirmative action programs, namely, "equal pay for equal work." The Equal
Pay Act does not require that all employees in a given job classification (for example, assistant professor) be paid the same wage. Rather, the Equal Pay Act
requires that wage differentials be based upon seniority, demonstrated merit, or,
what is probably the same thing as demonstrated merit, differential productivity.
The Equal Pay Act has resulted in a large number of suits, most of which charge
that women employees are being paid less than men employees of similar experience, merit, and productivity.[9] An important example is the Wheaton Glass
case (1970), in which the Wheaton Glass Company was found guilty of paying
male packing employees more than female packing employees doing the identical task.[10]

The Equal Pay Act and the concept of equal pay for equal work are both predicated on the judgment that it is possible to judge the equality (or inequality) of work effort. The Department of Labor, which is responsible for enforcing the Equal Pay Act, has suggested that the following four factors be used to make a determination about equality of work: (1) skill required, (2) effort involved, (3) job responsibility, and (4) repetitiveness of the task.[11] The problem here is that such factors refer primarily to the intrinsic character of the job itself, and do not address themselves to the question of whether the individual in that job is performing better, or worse, than others in the same job. For example, given that Professors Smith and Jones both have identical teaching, research, and service responsibilities, the crucial question relates to the performance of Professors Smith and Jones. It is often easier to establish job responsibilities and characteristics than to determine and evaluate differential productivity among the workers in a given job classification. This is particularly true in academia. Nearly all associate professors of economics in a given university have the same teaching, research, and service responsibilities in their jobs. Hence, there is ordinarily not great hand-wringing over the decision that most of or all these associate professors will be evaluated according to the same criteria. The major problem in academia is the evaluation of productivity itself. Is Professor John a better teacher (scholar) (colleague) than Professor Mary? This problem will be confronted again in Chapter 5 when the empirical evidence is presented.

Title VII of the Civil Rights Act of 1964

Title VII of the Civil Rights Act of 1964, as amended in 1972, prohibits discrimination because of race, color, religion, sex, or national origin in all employment practices, including hiring, firing, promotion, compensation, job classification and other terms, privileges, and conditions of employment. The coverage of Title VII is expansive: it includes all private firms where fifteen or more employees work for 20 or more weeks in a year, all educational institutions and labor unions, and all state and local government units.[12] Title VII also created the Equal Employment Opportunity Commission (EEOC) to administer and enforce Title VII. While the EEOC itself has no power to mete out penalties for noncompliance with Title VII or other laws and regulations, it has been given investigative power, the power to make recommendations to enforcement agencies, and the right to seek direct access to the courts. This last power frequently causes the EEOC to seek direct judicial relief and/or penalties in particular cases. When the EEOC discovers what it deems to be noncompliance with Title VII or subsequent laws or presidential executive orders, it ordinarily attempts to obtain voluntary compliance ("affirmative action") by the alleged offender.[a] Should the appropriate affirmative action

---

[a]The first affirmative action program officially approved by the federal government was presented by the McDonnell-Douglas Aircraft Corporation in the late 1960s.

not be forthcoming in the eyes of the EEOC, then the EEOC may recommend to the Department of Labor that the employer be considered to be in noncompliance and that some of or all the federal government's contracts with that employer be suspended or terminated. The Department of Labor has been given the power to implement penalties relating to the suspension or cancellation of contracts upon the recommendation of the EEOC or any other government civil rights agency.

As of November 1975, no university had lost any federal contract because of noncompliance with Title VII, although a host of threats, delays, and suspensions have been implemented by various agencies.[13] The court cases which have arisen because of challenges to Title VII have usually concentrated upon an exception written into Title VII which permits employers to discriminate on the basis of religion, sex, or national origin if such discrimination is ". . . reasonably necessary to the normal operation of that particular business."[14] Two of the most important cases involving sex discrimination issues have been *Phillips v. Martin Marietta Corporation*[15] and *Sprogis v. United Airlines.*[16] Both cases were brought under the provisions of Title VII; the Phillips decision dealt with sex discrimination in hiring, while the Sprogis decision concerned sex discrimination in job conditions. In both cases, the defendants challenged the basic constitutionality of Title VII and asserted that, in any case, any sex discrimination which occurred was necessary for the normal operation of their businesses and hence was protected under the exception noted above. These arguments were not accepted by the courts.

As implied above, the emphasis of Title VII enforcement is upon the consequences of discrimination rather than upon the intent of employers. That is, it is not deemed necessary for the EEOC to demonstrate that discrimination was either conscious or premeditated.[17] Instead, the EEOC need only produce a statistical survey which demonstrates that minorities and females are not employed at all job levels by a given firm in reasonable relation to their presence in the population and labor force, or that within a given job level equal pay is not granted to all employees performing equal work. Such a survey is considered to be *prima facie* evidence of discrimination as well as noncompliance with Title VII. The burden of proof falls, then, upon the employer to rebut the charge of discrimination. Pragmatically, this has meant that the employer either must find great fault with the data presented or must demonstrate a "compelling business necessity" for his or her actions. This latter phrase, "compelling business necessity," is the standard that the EEOC has imposed with respect to the provision of Title VII that allows discrimination in cases where it is necessary for the normal operation of the business. The interpretations of "compelling business necessity" by the EEOC and the courts have been very narrow and confining. The number of successful pleadings under this clause has been very small.

Often there may be pressure placed upon an employee not to bring formal charges against the employer concerning job discrimination. Even if the employer is innocent of the charge of discrimination, it is unlawful for the employer to bully or threaten the employee concerned in order to persuade that employee not to lodge formal charges with the EEOC or a similar body. The University of Maryland, Baltimore County, was accused, in October 1975, of threatening to fire Prof. Bette C. Thomas after she filed a complaint with the EEOC. The EEOC sought to obtain a permanent injunction against any such activities on the part of the university.[18]

Sex discrimination charges on the basis of Title VII are not easily demonstrated in academic cases. In *Green v. Board of Regents*, the plaintiff, an associate professor of English at Texas Technological University, charged that she had been systematically denied promotion to the rank of professor because of sex discrimination. The plaintiff had received her Ph.D. in 1955, had been at Texas Technological University since 1946, and had petitioned unsuccessfully for the rank of professor since 1962. She introduced considerable data concerning her own competence vis-à-vis that of her male colleagues, their relative salaries, and promotional histories. The plaintiff's attorneys cited *Reed v. Reed* as a basis for their claims of invidious sex discrimination. The court, however, denied the plaintiff relief on the ground that the plaintiff had received a fair hearing by reasonable authorities at all levels. Hence, sex discrimination could not be established.

Back Pay and Title VII

The intent of Title VII is not only to eliminate the practice of sex discrimination in employment, but also to provide equity for those who have been injured because of the past exercise of such discrimination. In the Timken Roller Bearing case, the court ruled that Title VII provides broad discretion to the courts in order to fashion orders designed to obtain relief from sex discrimination.[19] Specifically, the court has taken a counterfactual position in ruling that the intent of Title VII was that the court restore, so far as possible, the position of the victims of sex discrimination to where it would have been had no sex discrimination taken place. Thus, the court spoke unequivocally in favor of "back pay" awards to erase the effects of past sex discrimination in employment.

The effects of the Timken decision have been felt primarily outside academia. For example, on May 30, 1974, the American Telephone and Telegraph Company (AT&T) entered into a consent decree with the U.S. Department of Labor, the Department of Justice, and the EEOC. The agreement stipulated that AT&T will award an estimated $30 million in back pay and wage increases to over 25,000 managerial-level employees, plus an additional $7 million to another 7,000 employees (53 percent of whom were women) who were promoted to managerial jobs but paid less than the average male manager. Finally, AT&T agreed to pay another $14.9 million to 17,000 employees (58 percent of whom were women) who were promoted to managerial jobs, but who had been underpaid in their former nonmanagement positions.[20] In another large settlement, nine steel companies signed an agreement with the federal government to grant over $31 million in back pay.[21] In both the AT&T and the steel cases, the impact of the Timken decision caused the companies to sign consent decrees prior to a formal judicial decision.

It is the awards of back pay under Title VII that have stimulated the numerous affirmative action salary programs that have appeared in academia in recent years. While some of these programs (for example, the program at the University of California at Berkeley) have been constructed in direct response to the pressure and threats of federal agencies such as the EEOC, other programs (for example, that at Illinois State University) have been undertaken in anticipation of federal or judicial action that might otherwise take place.

An affirmative action salary program, whether or not judicially mandated, is not always without cost to nonminority, nonfemale faculty. In any given year, the budget dollars available to a university are generally finite. Similarly the dollars available for salary increments and salary adjustments are finite. This means that affirmative action salary increments to women and minority faculty may reduce the salary increments given to other faculty. This trade-off between affirmative action and non-affirmative-action salary increments, which may be dollar for dollar in a given year, is an important reason why affirmative action programs are often unpopular and become the target of the criticism of non-affirmative-action faculty members. As Betty Richardson has noted, ". . . faculty males, on the other hand, . . . now see that the central issue is salary and assume that the money given to women is being stolen from their own pockets."[22] Seldom have state legislatures or college governing boards actually given extra monies to the colleges and universities they control in order to further affirmative action. This means that affirmative action programs often are zero-sum games for male faculty. Monies given to female faculty for affirmative action purposes do not reduce male faculty salaries; however such monies ordinarily do reduce the salary increments given to male faculty. The legislatures and governing boards are therefore at least partially culpable for the unpopularity of affirmative action salary programs among nonminority, faculty.

Executive Orders 11,246 and 11,375

The coverage of Title VII has been supplemented by two presidential executive orders. The first, Executive Order 11,246 (1965), requires all federal contractors,[b] including universities that receive federal monies for research or other purposes, to sign an agreement not to discriminate against any employee on the

---

[b]The coverage is actually limited to federal contractors whose contracts exceed $50,000 in value and who employ 50 or more employees. All but a few colleges and universities fall under the coverage of orders 11,246 and 11,375.

basis of race, color, religion, or national origin. Such contractors must also file a written affirmative action program designed to eliminate any inequities that might exist. Executive Order 11,375 (1968) extended the coverage of order 11,246 to include discrimination on the basis of sex. The U.S. Department of Labor, as well as other enforcement agencies, has since issued detailed instructions concerning the administration and interpretation of these presidential executive orders.

To the untutored eye, it may appear as if Executive Orders 11,246 and 11,375 cover much the same ground as Title VII. The tone and requirements of the executive orders, however, are substantially different. Whereas Title VII forbids discrimination, the executive orders require that employers actively demonstrate that they are not discriminating. Further, the executive orders require an affirmative action program and a statement that the employer is not, and will not, discriminate in employment practices. Thus, the refusal of an employer to maintain an effective affirmative action program is sufficient reason to deny that employer federal contracts in the first instance. The executive orders make it unnecessary to wait to see if the employer does engage in discrimination.

The executive orders also created an Office of Federal Contract Compliance (OFCC) to monitor the requirements of the executive orders, Title VII, and the Equal Pay Act of 1963. The OFCC is charged with making determinations about the compliance of employers with existing law and the executive orders.

The executive orders were sweeping in another context. They required each major federal agency to maintain an office to deal with contract compliance after the fact, and also to make judgments about the eligibility of an employer for a contract before the fact. The executive orders require that no nonconstruction contract in excess of $1 million can be let without first ascertaining affirmative action compliance on the part of the employer desiring the contract.

The operational heart of the enforcement of Presidential Executive Orders 11,246 and 11,375 has been a system of "goals" and "quotas." That is, affirmative action programs are ordinarily required to contain specific goals in hiring and compensation that the employer agrees to seek and attain within a given time period. For example, as a part of the so-called Philadelphia Plan, which was an affirmative action hiring plan for Philadelphia-area trade unions, for each trade goals were set that indicated the percent of minority employment that was expected to be achieved by certain dates. For example, the ironworkers and their employers agreed to increase the percent of minority ironworkers from between 5 and 9 percent in 1970 to between 22 and 26 percent in 1973.[23] The agreement was hammered out by the Secretary of Labor personally in 1969. Protests by employers against the strictures of the affirmative action agreement resulted in a court suit which was decided in favor of the Secretary of Labor.[24]

The most publicized use of Executive Order 11,246 has occurred in the action taken by the Department of Health, Education, and Welfare (HEW) against the University of Texas in October 1975. For the first time, HEW has begun formal proceedings aimed at barring a university (in this case the University of Texas) from receiving any federal contracts. All other actions by HEW have involved threats, delays, and considerable negotiation.

The University of Texas case revolves around the allegation that Janet Rollins Berry, an assistant professor of history, was discriminated against in both salary and academic rank because of her sex. Professor Berry filed a formal complaint with the Office of Civil Rights of HEW in August 1971. HEW charged that Professor Berry's salary was approximately 36 percent lower than that paid to male faculty with similar qualifications. The University of Texas has formally requested a hearing on the proposed termination (the charges are no longer an issue). A hearing officer will be appointed, and the judgment of the hearing will be automatically reviewed by a group of five lawyers not in the employ of HEW. The ultimate appellant authority in the matter is the HEW Secretary, F. David Mathews.[25]

Revised Order Number 4

A host of interpretive rules and regulations have been issued pursuant to the Equal Pay Act of 1963, Title VII, and the Presidential Executive Orders 11,246 and 11,375. The most influential set of interpretations and instructions, however, has been Revised Order Number 4 which relates to the operation and requirements for affirmative action programs.[c] Either the Office of Federal Contract Compliance (OFCC) or an enforcement agency inside a particular federal department (for example, the Department of the Interior) may issue a finding that a contractor ". . . has no affirmative action program or that his program is not acceptable to the contracting officer."[26] The OFCC or other compliance agency will then give the contractor 30 days to show cause why the contractor's federal contracts should not be canceled or terminated. If the contractor does not show cause within the stated 30-day period, then the OFCC or compliance agency" . . . shall immediately issue a notice of proposed cancellation or termination of existing contracts or subcontracts and debarment from future contracts . . ."[27] The contractor then has 10 days in which to request a hearing. The results of the hearing will then govern the acceptability of the contractor for current and future federal contracts.

The most interesting and definitive sections of Revised Order Number 4 relate to hiring procedures. Revised Order Number 4 requires the affirmative action program of the employer to contain a "utilization analysis." This analysis is described as follows:

---

[c]Revised Order Number 4 was originally issued by the Office of Federal Contract Compliance, but can be utilized by other enforcement agencies.

An analysis of all major job classifications at the facility, with explanation of minorities or women are currently being underutilized in any
one or more job classifications (job "classification" herein meaning one
or a group of jobs having similar content, wage rates, and opportunities).
"Underutilization" is defined as having fewer minorities or women in a
particular job classification than would reasonably be expected by their
availability. In making the work force analysis, the contractor shall conduct such analysis separately for minorities and women.[28]

With respect to the utilization of women, and a judgment concerning underutilization, the following eight factors are to be considered:[29]

1. The size of the feamle unemployment force in the labor area sur-
    rounding the facility
2. The percentage of the female workforce as compared with the total
    workforce in the immediate labor area
3. The general availability of women having requisite skills in the im-
    mediate labor area
4. The availability of women having requisite skills in an area from which
    the contractor can reasonably recruit
5. The availability of women seeking employment in the labor or recruit-
    ment area of the contractor
6. The availability of promotable and transferable female employees within
    the contractor's organization
7. The existence of training institutions capable of training persons in the
    requisite skills
8. The degree of training which the contractor is reasonably able to under-
    take as a means of making all job classes available to women

Revised Order Number 4 also specifies that the contractor shall, in his affirmative action program, establish goals and timetables which detail both the contractor's affirmative action deficiencies and the schedule for eliminating those
deficiencies. The goals may not be ". . . rigid and inflexible quotas which must
be met. . . ."[30] However, there is expected on the part of the employer ". . .
good faith efforts to make his program work. . . ."[31] What is a good-faith effort,
however, is a matter of judgment. In the case of AT&T, cited earlier during the
discussion of back-pay awards, a good-faith effort was interpreted rather mech-
anically in terms of specific quotas and numerical goals that either were or were
not satisfied.

The demands of Revised Order Number 4 in terms of resources and data are
substantial. Support data necessary to evaluate and analyze the contractor's
affirmative action program must be compiled and maintained and should include,
but not be limited to, ". . . progression line charts, seniority rosters, applicant

flow data, and applicant rejection ratios indicating minority and sex status."[32] Additionally, an affirmative action officer shall be appointed by each contractor to encourage and accomplish affirmative action aims and goals. A total of twenty-nine specific duties (for example, an in-depth analysis of ". . . the total selection process including position descriptions, position titles, worker specifications, application forms, interview procedures, test administration, test validity, referral procedures, final selection process, and similar factors . . ."[33] are listed with respect to the affirmative action officer.

The EEOC Sex Discrimination Guidelines

It is apparent that the requirements of Revised Order Number 4 are both stringent and complicated. Revised Order Number 4, however, does not represent the whole of the regulations that an employer must follow with respect to affirmative action and discrimination. For example, in the area of sex discrimination, the EEOC has issued its own set of guidelines which federal contractors must satisfy. (Note once again that nearly every college and university is a "federal contractor" according to the definitions set forth in the laws, presidential executive orders, and guidelines cited above.) The EEOC guidelines specifically warn the employer against refusing to hire women because of assumptions about the ". . . comparative employment characteristics of women in general. For example, the assumption that the turnover rate among women is higher than among men."[34] The import of this warning is considerable. Even if it is believed that job turnover rates among women employees are higher than among men employees, it is not acceptable in the eyes of the EEOC to refuse to hire women employees on that basis. Sex may not be used as a generalized screening device. Instead, each employee, whether male or female, must be considered as a separate entity and evaluated as a prospective employee without reference to sex.

The EEOC guidelines are more restrictive than Revised Order Number 4 where sex characteristics are concerned. The employer is not permitted to consider suppositions about job performance which are characterized only on the basis of sex. By way of contrast, the employer may consider suppositions concerning turnover, productivity, and so forth, which are differentiated on the basis of a characteristic such as experience or previous education. Hence, it is possible to refuse to hire a given class of individuals because it is believed that this class of individual is not qualified to hold the job in question. A university degree, for example, might become a proxy for adequate training. An Ivy League university is permitted to refuse to hire professors who do not possess a bachelor's degree if the Ivy League university believes that non-bachelor's-degree holders do not function well as professors. At the same time, it is not permissible for an Ivy League university to refuse to hire women faculty in general, or a particular woman faculty in a given case, because the Ivy League university believes that women faculty are more often absent, less productive, and less pleasing colleagues than men faculty. Empirical evidence of a very strong and convincing variety must be produced in support of any blanket prohibition upon hiring which is based upon sex. At no time in its existence, however, has the EEOC indicated that it places any credence whatsoever in any empirical evidence purporting to demonstrate differences between the turnover, productivity, and performance of men and women faculty.

The reluctance of the EEOC to be convinced by empirical evidence, casual or otherwise, that differences exist between the turnover, productivity, and performance of men and women faculty members is a defensible position on several counts. First, there is impressively little reliable evidence concerning such matters. (The scraps of evidence that are available, however, will be considered in Chapter 4.) Second, the empirical evidence that is extant may be deficient. If women faculty are actually found to have greater job turnover and to be less productive as scholars, it may nonetheless be the case that the observed differentials are due to sex discrimination which biases evaluations or which actually alters and distorts performances. The possibility that identical behavior and performances by men and women faculty may be perceived differently is real and will be considered in Chapter 5.

Title IX Regulations

The most recent set of federal regulations relating to affirmative action and sex discrimination is that issued by the Department of Health, Education, and Welfare to implement Title IX of the Education Amendments Act of 1972. Except for very limited exceptions, Title IX regulations apply to activities of a college or university when that college or university receives federal funds. It also applies to elementary and secondary schools. Title IX regulations require the absence of sex discrimination in admissions, athletics, campus organizations, use of physical facilities, curricular materials, and employment of all kinds.

The major impact of Title IX regulations is upon students and the use of physical facilities. In particular, the effects of Title IX regulations have been felt most in the area of intramural and intercollegiate athletics, where the time, facilities, coaching, and budgets allotted to women have been but a small fraction of those devoted to men. The employment regulations are a virtual restatement of Title VII law and EEOC regulations. Nonetheless, one important area of compensation, namely, fringe benefits, is highlighted in Title IX regulations. Fringe benefit compensation has been given scant attention in other laws and regulations. Title IX regulations specifically require that ". . . employers must provide either equal contributions to or equal benefits under pension plans for male and female employees; as to pregnancy, leave and fringe benefits to pregnant employees must be offered in the same manner as are leave and benefits to temporarily disabled employees."[35] This means, for example, that benefits which favor married men, or heads of families, are not permissible. Further, it means that pregnancy must be treated in the same fashion as a sickness would be treated for a male employee. In the usual academic case, this implies a paid leave for the female professor at or around the time of birth.

Title IX regulations took effect on July 21, 1975, and have not yet been subjected to the inevitable court tests.[36] An examination of judicial attitudes with respect to other affirmative action regulations, for example, Presidential Executive Orders 11,246 and 11,375, leads to the prediction that the constitutionality of the Title IX regulations will be upheld at all levels.

Changes in the Wind

College administrators have long complained that the federal government's affirmative action requirements have been drawn up with an industrial situation in mind. The guidelines, academic administrators charge, are unsuited to an academic situation and are extremely burdensome in nature. Secretary of Labor John T. Dunlop, who is a professor of economics and a former dean at Harvard University, has stated that he is ". . . unsympathetic with the requirement that universities be forced to adopt the massive . . . statistical approach . . ." to justifying their affirmative action efforts.[37] Dunlop has proposed that the affirmative action guidelines of the various federal agencies be rewritten with an eye to simplifying their language and data requirements. To that end, Secretary Dunlop held a series of hearings in August 1975, concerning affirmative action programs. Testimony at the hearings was particularly invited from those who would comment upon ". . . the special circumstances, if any, in higher education which might suggest alternative affirmative-action approaches and the nature of such approaches."[38]

One interested party in the affirmative action arena has been the Carnegie Council on Policy Studies in Higher Education. The Carnegie Council has argued in favor of a special set of affirmative action regulations tailored to academia. There is precedent for such an action. Special industry agreements concerning affirmative action have been constructed and approved in steel, tires, and paper. Additionally, a special set of regulations has been drawn up for a single company, AT&T.

The Carnegie Council has issued a set of twenty-seven recommendations concerning affirmative action programs in colleges and universities. The recommendations include:

1. Goals and timetables should be set for the hiring of instructors and assistant professors, but not for associate professor and professor ranks.

2. The individual college or university should decide whether stated affirmative action goals should apply at a departmental, collegial, or universitywide level.

3. A particular institution should be exempted from stating detailed goals, requirements, and so forth, when it can demonstrate that the proportion of women and minority faculty on its staff already corresponds closely to the proportion of women and minority faculty actually available.

4. The Department of Health, Education, and Welfare, and not the Department of Labor, should deal with academia in the area of affirmative action programs.

5. Increased emphasis should be placed upon the long-run supply of women and minority faculty. Each institution with graduate programs should develop a supply plan designed to provide a maximum number of opportunities for women and minorities in graduate education.

6. Separate affirmative action guidelines should be created for faculty which differ from those which apply to staff and administrators.

7. Colleges and universities should be reimbursed for the substantial expenditures they must make for record keeping and implementation of affirmative action.

8. The federal government should, by 1980, review the progress of affirmative action and decide what requirements are still needed at particular institutions. "The presumption should be in favor of disengagement as soon as reasonably possible."[39]

The Department of Health, Education, and Welfare has muddied the affirmative action waters recently by issuing a memorandum that is directed at the problem of reverse discrimination in hiring. A frequent charge articulated against affirmative action programs is that they require unconstitutional discrimination against male, nonminority faculty members. Given a quota or goal which expresses a desire to hire additional women faculty, will a university intentionally pass over more qualified men applicants in favor of less qualified women applicants?

Peter E. Holmes, Director of the Department of Health, Education, and Welfare's Office for Civil Rights, has interpreted the December, 1974, memorandum as saying that ". . . colleges and universities are entitled to select the most qualified candidate, without regard to race, sex or ethnicity, for any position."[40] Further, he asserted that the memorandum allows the colleges and universities, not the federal government, to determine what constitutes the qualifications for any particular position.

The Department of Health, Education, and Welfare memorandum, which was sent to over 3,000 college and university presidents, cited the following case as an improper interpretation of affirmative action requirements:

> For the past four years, the Mathematics Department of X University
> has been operating under an affirmative action program. Although its
> goal for hiring women was established at 20 percent over a five-year
> period, during the past four years, each of the four vacancies have been
> filled by a male. At an annual professional association conference, the
> department chairman informed a male applying for a fifth vacancy that
> he could not be given consideration regardless of his qualifications
> because Federal regulations require the department to fill the position
> with a woman.[41]

This interpretation, states the memorandum, is improper. One may not designate
such an academic opening as being a position for women only, or even designate
that women would be preferred candidates for the opening.

The Department of Health, Education, and Welfare memorandum and the
Department of Labor hearings have led many observers to charge that the federal
government is waivering in its support of affirmative action programs and nondiscriminatory principles. Walter J. Leonard, the affirmative action officer at
Harvard University, has complained that the memorandum and the hearings
might be used by ". . . a number of institutions which have done nothing as an
opportunity to relieve colleges of the responsibility to perform . . . .[42] Other
institutions, he feels, may see in these developments a ". . . way to defend what
they have not done."[43]

The only concrete development which has come from the memorandum and
the hearings has been a new reporting form which institutions may use to report
their affirmative action activities. The data requirements of affirmative action
programs and the interference with their internal operations continue, however,
to be sore spots with many colleges and universities.

It should be noted at this point that by far the greatest number of complaints concerning affirmative action has arisen in relation to the hiring and
promotional process. Fewer complaints have been generated by affirmative
action salary-increment programs. This reflects the fact that the data requirements for a study of affirmative action in hiring are immense and perhaps in-
superable. Further, the success of affirmative action programs in hiring and
promotion can be effectively observed only in the long run. By way of contrast,
affirmative action salary programs require less data, and are more concise and
short-run in most respects. Either salaries monies are given or they are not. The
results can be monitored within the context of a given year instead of requiring
a period of 30+ years for evaluation, as in the case of the affirmative action
hiring plan of the University of California at Berkeley.

At the same time that there is visible and influential opposition to the
requirements and operation of affirmative action programs, the Equal Rights
Amendment to the Constitution is apparently stalled short of approval. The
Equal Rights Amendment states that it is unconstitutional to deny or abridge

someone's rights or equality under the law on the basis of sex. It has been passed by both the Senate and the House of Representatives, and has been ratified by 34 of the needed 38 states. Several of the states that have given their approval to the amendment, however, have since withdrawn that approval, and several other states have been contemplating the ways and means to do the same. The legal status of the ratification procedure is then in doubt.

The plight of the Equal Rights Amendment is another manifestation of the type of opposition that has developed with respect to affirmative action programs. Fundamental changes in the social and economic roles of females have generated increasingly vociferous opposition from sources both inside and outside academia. At the same time, however, it would be incorrect to ascribe sexist motives to all the opposition to affirmative action programs. For, as the Carnegie Council has noted, ". . . seldom has a good cause spawned such a badly developed series of federal mechanisms."[44] The affirmative action law and regulations are complex, frustrating, and expensive to satisfy.

Summary and Evaluation

Affirmative action programs and laws and regulations against sex discrimination in employment are here to stay. Beginning with the Equal Pay Act of 1963, a profusion of laws and regulations have been instituted which are designed to eliminate the practice and effects of sex discrimination in employment. Any employer of importance now maintains an affirmative action program. During fiscal year 1974, the EEOC handled 55,885 cases involving sex discrimination and affirmative action.[45] Cash benefits totaling $56.2 million were paid to over 49,000 employees because of the EEOC rulings.[46] Additionally, as of August 1974, the EEOC had obtained 38 consent decrees in which employers agreed under judicial supervision (and threat of penalty) to undertake affirmative action.[47] The aforementioned AT&T consent decree is one of the most publicized of such actions.

That affirmative action programs have inspired storms of opposition is hardly surprising, for, as Theodore Caplow has noted in his classic study, *The Academic Marketplace*, academic employment and reward structures are often featured by croneyism and inside, informal relationships which are antithetical to affirmative action.[48] Betty Richardson has labeled this the "Old Boys Club" phenomenon.[49] Sexist practices are strongly entrenched in academia and are not easily altered.[50]

Nonetheless, it has become apparent to many observers that affirmative action programs are far too complicated to administer efficiently. The programs attempt too much and require far too much in the way of resources in order to satisfy the dictates of the law and the interpretive regulations. Additionally, it is possible that a university that rigidly follows the maze of affirmative action guidelines may find itself guilty of reverse discrimination against male, nonminority faculty, or it may be forced to behave inefficiently in a strict economic context. It is reasonable to hypothesize that given particular university's budget constraint and circumstances, the best possible professor may not be hired because of affirmative action; and the dispensation of financial rewards and promotions encouraged by affirmative action may not necessarily reward the most productive faculty members. Further, many of the affirmative action programs which actually have met the approval of the various federal agencies may be of doubtful value. A recent study by the General Accounting Office indicated that over 20 percent of the affirmative action plans approved by federal agencies were deficient and did not comply with existing law and regulations.[51]

The position of affirmative action programs today is accurately portrayed by the statement "damned if you do, damned if you don't." Laws and regulations have been written and, in some cases, enforced. Those who administer these laws and regulations can be assured that they will be subjected to criticism whether they rigidly enforce these laws and regulations or whether they allow affirmative action to wither from "benign neglect." The empirical evidence reported in Chapter 5 relates to the former case where affirmative action has been aggressive and active in the context of the legal background cited in this chapter.

3

Theories of Sex Discrimination

Practical men, who believe themselves to be quite exempt from any
intellectual influence, are usually the slaves of some defunct economist.
Madmen in authority, who hear voices in the air, are distilling their
frenzy from some academic scribbler or a few years back.

Affirmative action programs have arisen because of the alleged existence of
sex discrimination in employment. In the absence of sex discrimination in employment, there is no persuasive reason why affirmative action programs should
exist. An important part of any study of affirmative action programs is, therefore, a demonstration that sex discrimination can or does exist. This chapter is
concerned with the a priori basis for sex discrimination. Why does sex discrimination occur? What conditions are most conducive to its occurrence? Who
are the winners (losers) when sex discrimination occurs?

Economic theories of sex discrimination are in fact hybrid offshoots of
theories of racial discrimination. There has been very little theorizing with
respect to the economics of sex discrimination per se. Rather, theories of sex
discrimination typically fit in the mold of racial discrimination models in which
whites discriminate against blacks. Sex discrimination models amend this to deal
with the case where men discriminate against women. This adaptation is, as we
shall see, not always appropriate.

Our tour of theories of sex discrimination will commence with the standard
neoclassical theory of discrimination as propounded by Gary Becker in his well-
known *The Economics of Discrimination*.[1] This basic model will be extended
and criticized. In particular, the impact of imperfect market structures upon
sex discrimination will be considered. Finally, the Marxian approach to sex discrimination will be detailed and critiqued.

The Competitive Trade Model of Becker

The seminal work in the area of discrimination has been produced by Gary
Becker.[2] Becker analyzes two independent societies, one white and one black,
which trade with each other. As applied to sex discrimination,[3] the Becker

J. M. Keynes, *General Theory of Employment, Interest, and Money* (New York:
Harcourt, Brace and Company), p. 383.

tradition deals with a male society and a female society which are independent of each other. The male society is presumed to be capital-rich, and the female society is presumed to have abundant labor. Free trade in inputs between the two societies would increase the output of both societies and lead to a position on the contract curve in an Edgeworth-Bowley box. Output maximization is equivalent to utility maximization because each individual, male or female, seeks to maximize a utility function which has output as its single argument.

Figure 3-1 illustrates a Becker type world in terms of an Edgeworth-Bowley box. The isoquant map of the male society is given by $l_1^m, l_2^m, \ldots, l_n^m$, while the isoquant map of the female society is given by $l_1^f, l_2^f, \ldots, l_n^f$. The

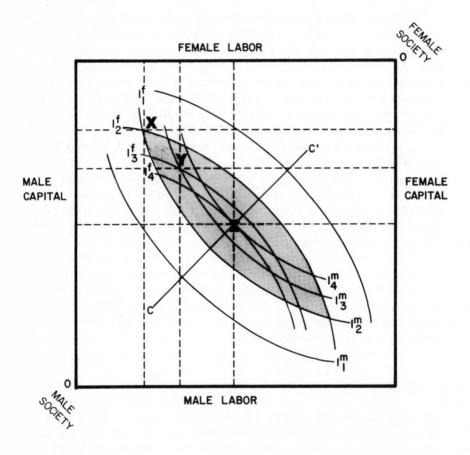

Figure 3-1. Edgeworth-Bowley Box Interpretation of Becker's Model of Discrimination.

initial endowment of capital (K) and labor (L) is given by point X in Figure 3-1. Male society has abundant capital, and the independent female society has abundant labor.

At point X in Figure 3-1, male isoquant l_2^m is intersected by female isoquant l_2^f. Hence, at this point the marginal rate of technical substitution between capital and labor in the male society is not the same as the marginal rate of technical substitution between the same two inputs in the female society. That is, $-dK/dL$ in the male society is greater than the corresponding $-dK/dL$ in the female society. This is apparent because the slope of l_2^m is steeper than the slope of l_2^f at point X.

Whenever two isoquants intersect, it is possible, by means of free trade in inputs, to move away from that point of intersection and thereby increase the output of both parties to the trade. It is clear, however, that if both parties to the trading process are knowledgeable, and if neither is coerced or forced to trade, then the male society will never accept a trade which would place it on an isoquant which results in less output than that given by l_2^m. Similarly, the female society will balk at any trade which would place it on an isoquant inferior to l_2^f. These two isoquants, l_2^m and l_2^f, enclose the range of feasible trades that is likely to take place between the male and female societies. This "football" is darkened in Figure 3-1.

Many possible trades could occur which would place both societies in a position preferred to that at point X. One such trade would result in a movement from point X to point Y. At point Y, both the male and the female societies are better off in their own eyes. The male society has advanced to isoquant l_3^m and the female society to isoquant l_3^f. l_3^m and l_3^f intersect at point Y, however, and therefore further output-increasing trades (both societies) are possible. Given voluntary trade and knowledgeable traders, trade will cease when the contract curve (labelled CC' in Figure 3-1) is reached. The contract curve CC' contains all points where the marginal technical rate of substitution between capital and labor is the same for both traders. Once the contract curve is reached, any further trading, even a movement along the contract curve CC', will increase the output of one society while reducing the output of the other. It can also be seen that any position off the contract curve is inferior to at least one position on the contract curve. Hence, no trade will occur which would move the two traders from a point on CC' to a point off CC'.

The contract curve CC' in Figure 3-1 is the locus of Pareto optimal points. This means that any movement in any direction will decrease the output of at least on of the traders. Pareto optimality implies that a tangency (rather than an intersection) exists between an isoquant of the male society and an isoquant of the female society. For example, at point Z on contract curve CC', male society isoquant l_4^m is tangent to female society isoquant l_4^f. No further trade is beneficial once the contract curve is reached at a point such as Z because the marginal rate of technical substitution between capital and labor is the same for both the male and the female societies.

The trading of inputs between the independent male and female societies is utility-maximizing given the Beckerian connection between output and utility. Male society trades its abundant capital for the female society's abundant labor, and both societies are better off.

Enter now sex discrimination against the female society. Assume that men are willing to pay a premium in order to avoid associating with women. Specifically, men desire to avoid importing and using female labor. This implies that men will therefore export less of their male capital to the female society. The result is the attainment of a position inferior to point Z in Figure 3-1. Point Y is one such possibility which involves male society refusing to import female labor. In the context of a university, point Y illustrates male faculty refusing to hire female faculty. Consequently, both the male society and the female society end up on lower isoquants than in the nondiscriminatory situation. Male society attains isoquant l_3^m (which is inferior to l_4^m), while female society attains isoquant l_3^f (which is inferior to l_4^f). This is a central finding of Becker, namely, that when actual discrimination occurs, the discriminator ". . . must, in fact, either pay or forfeit income for this privilege."[4] This finding, as we shall soon see, hinges crucially upon the assumptions made about the wage elasticities of supply and demand for both male and female labor.

Becker now introduces discrimination into the trade model. If an individual has a "taste for discrimination," says Becker, then he must ". . . act as if he were willing to pay something either directly or in the form of a reduced income, to be associated with some persons instead of others."[5] Becker chooses to measure the effects of discrimination by means of a "discrimination coefficient" (DC), which is analogous to a tariff in the area of international trade. He states,

> Suppose an employer were faced with the money wage rate Π of a particular factor; he is assumed to act as if $\Pi (1 + d_i)$ were the net wage rate, with d_i as his DC against this factor. An employee, offered the money wage rate Π_i for working with this factor, acts as if $\Pi_i (1 - d_i)$ were the net wage rate.[6]

The salient point of Becker's analysis is that the discriminator pays a penalty for the discrimination. In the context of the Edgeworth-Bowley box of Figure 3-1, this means that both the male society and the female society attain a position which is inferior to that given by point Z. For example, assume that male society has an aversion to female labor such that the male society is unwilling to trade substantial amounts of its capital for female labor. If such is the case, then point Z in Figure 3-1 will not be reached. Instead, an inferior point, such as Y, will be attained. The cost to each of the trading parties is the decreased production associated with isoquants l_3^m and l_3^f rather than l_4^m and l_4^f. The character of the misallocation and suboptimization is illustrated by the fact that (at point Y)

$$\text{(male)} \qquad \text{(female)}$$

$$\frac{MP_L}{MP_K} \quad \neq \quad \frac{MP_L}{MP_K} \tag{3.1}$$

That is, the ratio of the marginal productivities of labor and capital is not the same in the male society as it is in the female society.

The discrimination solution at point Y in Figure 3-1 could be arrived at for other reasons. For example, it could be the case that the male society possesses monopoly power and wishes to force a particular trade upon the female society.

The assumption of a taste for discrimination on the part of the male society alters the original Becker assumptions in one very concrete fashion. The male society now has both a taste for output and a taste for discrimination. The female society, however, has only a taste for output. As Madden has demonstrated, the contract curve in such a situation need not be linear.[7]

The most complete statement and elaboration of a Becker-type model of discrimination has been provided by Arrow.[8] Arrow introduces such innovations as assuming that not all firms have the same taste for discrimination, nonconvexities of indifference curves, and imperfect information. For our purposes, however, the work of Becker suffices.

The Assumptions Underpining the
Becker Model

The Becker model of discrimination is based upon eight explicit and implicit assumptions:

1. The male and female societies are independent.
2. Only two factor inputs, L and K, exist.
3. The male and female societies trade L and K, but not the single output.
4. The production functions in both the male and the female societies are linear homogeneous.
5. The male society is assumed to be capital-rich, while the female society is assumed to be labor-rich.
6. The input supply curves of the male and female societies are infinitely elastic with respect to wages.
7. The male society has a taste both for output and for discrimination, while the female society has a taste only for output.

8. Perfect competition reigns throughout such that all resources and factor inputs are perfectly mobile between the male and female societies.[9]

We will shortly spend considerable time considering the implications of variations in assumptions 6 and 8, dealing with factor input supply elasticities and perfect competition, respectively. We can examine the effect of relaxing assumptions 3 and 4. The Becker production function is one in which a single output is produced with two inputs. Assume now that two outputs exist, of which one is produced in a labor-intensive fashion and the other in a capital-intensive fashion. Presumably the female society would specialize in the production of the labor-intensive good, while the male society would specialize in the production of the capital-intensive good.[10] The female society could then trade this labor-intensive good to the male society for the capital-intensive good of the male society. If female labor is discriminated against, then there will be a much greater tendency to trade outputs rather than inputs. This will emphasize the specialization of the female society in the labor-intensive good. Regardless, if there is free trade between the male and female societies in the two goods, then factor price equalization will occur. This is a standard international trade result, although it is based upon possibly debatable assumptions.[11] Factor price equalization means that it will be very difficult for the male society to discriminate successfully against the female society. Hence, in order to assume that successful discrimination can occur, it is necessary to break away from the conditions that produce factor price equalization. For example, successful discrimination against the female society is not precluded if trade in goods is precluded, if increasing returns to scale exist, or if the two goods are produced with the same capital-to-labor ratios.

Becker's work is also based upon the assumption of a linear homogeneous production function. As Madden has shown, this assumption can be dispensed with as long as trade in commodities is not allowed and there is only one commodity being produced.[12] When trade is confined to factor inputs and only one output is produced, then the quantity of factors traded is not affected. However, if trade in multiple goods is allowable and increasing returns to scale exist for both societies, then the end result is that there is total specialization of the female society in the labor-intensive good or total specialization of the male society in the capital-intensive good. If the absolute specialization occurs in the male society, then the terms of trade between the commodities will turn in favor of the male society. The reverse is true when it is the female society that engages in absolute specialization.

The Introduction of Imperfect Competition

The Becker model assumes perfect competition in both the input and the output markets. The most frequent exception taken to this assumption involves the counterassumption of monopsony in the factor input markets for labor. A *monopsonist* is an employer who faces an upward sloping supply-of-labor curve. This situation can be contrasted to the infinitely wage-elastic supply curve of labor which holds in Becker's analysis.

The classic monopsonist of economic theory is a large firm. General Motors, for example, has probably bid up wages in the Detroit area when it has expanded its production and the area economy has been at or near full employment. Monopsony power can also derive from the real or tacit collusion of a group of firms. Trade associations such as the International Air Transport Association often behave in a monopsonistic fashion in the factor input markets.

The exercise of monopsony power, by itself, has no implications for sex discrimination. If, however, the monopsonist observes that the relevant labor market is segmented into two or more groups of workers, each of which has a different wage elasticity of supply for labor, then it is possible for the monopsonist to engage in profitable monopsonistic discrimination. The sex-discriminating monopsonist model is therefore predicated upon three necessary conditions. First, monopsony power itself must be present. Second, it must be possible for the monopsonist to segment the labor market between male and female employees. Third, the male and female segments of the labor market must have differing wage elasticities of supply for labor.

A general monopsony model resulting in discrimination has been discussed or developed by several writers, including Robinson,[13] Bronfenbrenner,[14] Thurow,[15] and Madden.[16] Madden's work explicitly relates to sex discrimination. The model which follows is therefore more in the Madden tradition, although the model's antecedents are to be found particularly in Robinson and Bronfenbrenner.

Assume a firm which faces a product demand function of the form

$$P = f(Q) \tag{3.2}$$

where P = price of output per unit
Q = output in units

The firm's production function is given by

$$Q = f(M, F) \tag{3.3}$$

where M = units of male labor
F = units of female labor

Both the male and female labor supplies are assumed to depend upon the wage rate paid that type of labor:

$$M = f(W_M)$$ (3.4)

$$F = f(W_F)$$ (3.5)

where W_M = wage paid to male labor
W_F = wage paid to female labor

Profit maximization requires, in the case of monopsony, that the marginal contribution of each particular type of labor be equated to the marginal expense of hiring that type of labor. Given perfect competition in the output market,[a] the firm must satisfy Equations (3.6) and (3.7):[17]

$$VMP_i = ME_i$$ (3.6)

$$VMP_i = W(1 + 1/\theta_i)$$ (3.7)

where VMP_i = value of the marginal product of input i
ME_i = Marginal expense of hiring an additional unit of input i
MP_i = marginal product of input i
θ_i = wage elasticity of supply for input i such that
$\theta = (\partial X_i / \partial W_i) \ (W_i / X_i)$

Equation (3.7) can be modified to take into account the differing wage elasticities of supply for male and female labor:

$$VMP_M = W_M(1 + 1/\theta_M)$$ (3.8)

$$VMP_F = W_F(1 + 1/\theta_F)$$ (3.9)

Given perfect substitutability between male and female labor, it follows that the firm cannot be in equilibrium unless $VMP_M = VMP_F$. The first-order condition for profit maximization in the presence of a wage-discriminating monopsonist can therefore be expressed as

$$W_M(1 + 1/\theta_M) = W_F(1 + 1/\theta_F)$$ (3.10)

The monopsonistic firm which satisfies Equation (3.10) will maximize its profit. It will also engage in sex discrimination in wages if $\theta_M \neq \theta_F$. Assume,

---

[a]Given imperfect competition in the output market, the firm pays attention to the marginal revenue product of input i (MRP_i) rather than VMP_i. Hence, Equation (3.6) becomes $MRP_i = MC_i$, and Equation (3.7) becomes $MR \cdot MP_i = W(1 + 1/\theta_i)$.

for example, that $\theta_M > \theta_F$.[18] Then, it follows that $W_M > W_F$, and female labor which produces a given marginal product receives a lower wage than male labor that produces the same marginal product, because male labor has a higher wage elasticity of supply than female labor. In general, the type of labor which has the higher wage elasticity of supply receives the higher wage. The type of labor that has the lower wage elasticity of supply receives the lower wage and is subjected to discrimination.

The contrast between the profit-maximizing solution for a price-discriminating firm with two customers and the wage-discriminating firm with two separable types of labor is instructive. In the price-discrimination model, the higher price is charged to the customer with the least price-elastic demand. By way of contrast, in the wage-discrimination model, the higher wage is paid to the type of labor that possesses the most wage-elastic supply of labor. Note that the firm maximizes profit in both instances by engaging in discrimination. Hence, the monopsony model, when combined with discrimination, predicts that sex discrimination against female labor in terms of wages is profitable. This is the opposite of the Becker prediction, namely, that discrimination lowers output and profits.

The wage-discriminating monopsonist argument can also be illustrated graphically. The *VMP* curve in Figure 3-2 illustrates the firm's demand curve for male and labor. Male and female labor are again assumed to be perfect substitutes for each other. Profit maximization requires that the firm equate the marginal expense of each input (ME_M and ME_F, respectively) to the *VMP* that is produced jointly by male and female labor. It is not possible to draw a separate *VMP* curve for male labor unless one assumes a given amount of female labor, and vice versa. Hence, the firm can be visualized as deciding to hire that amount of labor where $\Sigma ME = ME_M = ME_F = VMP$ because the output is jointly produced by perfectly substitutable male and female labor. Applying that condition to Figure 3-2, we find that the firm will hire OO_M units of male labor which it will pay wage OW_M; it will hire OW_F units of female labor which it will pay wage OW_F and it will hire a total of $OQ_M + OQ_F = OQ_T$ units of labor overall. Once again, we see that female labor receives a lower wage because its wage elasticity of labor supply is less than that of male labor.

The "Overcrowding" Variant

Almost 60 years have passed since the original exposition of the "overcrowding" hypothesis by a group of British economists.[19] The hypothesis states that societal attitudes, monopsony power, and prejudice act to limit the employment of women in certain occupations. Hence, other occupations are characterized by an "overcrowding" of women job candidates. The surfeit of women in these occupations drives down the marginal productivities and wages of women in

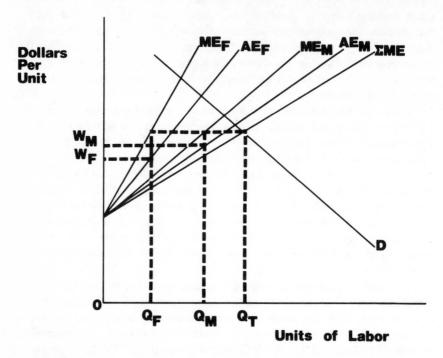

Figure 3-2. Profit Maximization by a Wage-Discriminating Monopsonist

these occupations. The absence of women in other occupations increases the marginal productivities and wages of men in those occupations. The wage differential, then, is not due to differences in the training or ability of men and women workers. Rather, it is due to the exercise of sexist attitudes, monopsony power, and prejudice which results in women being forced into certain occupations.

There is empirical evidence in support of the contention that women are disproportionately represented in certain occupations which are characterized by low marginal productivities and low wages. For example, Valerie Oppenheimer has found gross disparities between expected and actual female employment in various occupations.[20] Females tend to be greatly overrepresented in certain occupations (for example, secretarial services) and underrepresented in other occupations (for example, engineers). The expected employment of females is derived as a function of training and labor force participation.

The overcrowding of female labor into certain occupations will decrease wages of females in those occupations. At the same time, however, there will be a smaller number of females competing for jobs in other occupations, and this will tend to increase the wages of females in these other occupations. Whether or not women as a class are worse off can be evaluated in terms of: (1) the change, if any, in the total wage payment made to female employees in all occupations, and (2) the change, if any, in the proportion of total income generated in each of these occupations which goes to females.

With regard to (1) above, the wage elasticity of demand for female and male labor is crucial. Suppose the demand for female labor is wage-elastic in the overcrowded occupations. This will mean that an influx of female labor will cause wage rates in these occupations to fall less than proportionately with respect to the increase in labor supply. The effect is to increase the total wage payment made to female labor in these occupations. On the other hand, if the wage elasticity of demand for labor in these occupations is inelastic, then an influx of female labor will drive down wage rates disproportionately with respect to the increase in labor supply. This would decrease the total wage payment made to female labor in these occupations.

In occupations where female workers are underrepresented, a wage-elastic demand will result in wages being higher than otherwise; however, the increase in wages due to the exodus of female workers into such occupations will be less than proportionate to the decreased employment of females. Hence, the total wage payment made to female labor in such an instance would decline. In the reverse case, where the demand for labor in such occupations is wage-inelastic, the total wage payment made to female labor will increase.

Table 3-1 summarizes these findings. We see that the total wage bill paid to female labor will actually increase due to overcrowding if the wage elasticity of demand for female labor is elastic in the overcrowded occupations and inelastic in the underrepresented occupations. Conversely, the total wage bill paid to female labor will decrease because of overcrowding it the wage elasticity of demand for female labor is inelastic in the overcrowded occupations and elastic in the underrepresented occupations. When both demands in both types of occupations are either wage-elastic or wage-inelastic, the effect upon the total wage bill paid to females is a priori unclear. The answer in this case depends upon the strength of the two competing effects, which in turn depends upon the

Table 3-1
The Overcrowding Hypothesis and the Total Female Wage Bill

	Effect of Overcrowding on Female Wage Bill in	
Wage Elasticity of Demand	Overcrowded Occupations	Underrepresented Occupations
Elastic	Increased	Decreased
Unit elastic	Remains constant	Remains constant
Inelastic	Decreased	Increased

proportion of female labor that is present in the overcrowded occupations vis-à-
vis the underrepresented occupations. Note that this analysis holds constant
such factors as cyclical changes in demand for the products produced by each
occupation, the nonmonetary characteristics of jobs, and so forth.

With regard to evaluative criterion (2) above, whether or not the share of
female labor in total income decreases or increases because of overcrowding
depends upon the elasticity of substitution between female labor and other
factor inputs. Assume a production function of the form $Q = f(M, F)$, as before.
The elasticity of substitution between male and female labor is given by
$\sigma = (\partial M/\partial F) \cdot (W_M/W_F)$. The ratio W_M/W_F will increase if the overall effect
of overcrowding drowns out the effect of underrepresentation. Overcrowding
tends to depress female wages, while underrepresentation tends to increase
female wages. The ratio W_M/W_F will decline when the overcrowding is less than
the effect of underrepresentation.

Table 3-2 summarizes the effect of each of these developments upon the
male and female shares of total income when $\sigma > 1.00$, $\sigma < 1.00$, and $\sigma = 1.00$.
Note that when W_M/W_F increases (the a priori expectation), the share of female
labor in total income will increase (decrease) (remain constant) accordingly as
the elasticity of substitution is greater than (less than) (equal to) 1. When male
and female labor are deemed to be perfect substitutes, then $\sigma \to \infty$. This directly
implies that overcrowding will increase the share of female labor in total income,
while it will decrease male labor's share of the same pie. Hence, in terms of
income-distributional consequences, deliberate propagation of overcrowding of
females in certain occupations will actually decrease the share of male labor in
total income when a high degree of substitutability exists between male and
female labor. In fact, the degree of substitutability is far less than infinite, and
may be less than 1 in many occupations. In such a case, a deliberate male policy
of forcing females into certain occupations will increase the share of male labor
in total income.

Table 3-2
**The Elasticity of Substitution and the Effect of Overcrowding upon Male
and Female Factor Shares**

Net Effect of Overcrowding upon wages	*The Effect of a Change in (W_M/W_F) upon Male and Female Relative Income Shares When*		
	$\sigma > 1.00$	$\sigma = 1.00$	$\sigma < 1.00$
$\dfrac{W_M}{W_F}$ ↑	*M*'s share ↓ *F*'s share ↑	*M*'s share ↔ *F*'s share ↔	*M*'s share ↑ *F*'s share ↓
$\dfrac{W_M}{W_F}$ ↓	*M*'s share ↑ *F*'s share ↓	*M*'s share ↔ *F*'s share ↔	*M*'s share ↓ *F*'s share ↑

The previous discussion of the effects of overcrowding upon wage bills and upon the distribution of income did not take into consideration the resource-allocation aspects of overcrowding. Overcrowding, as Bergmann has demonstrated, probably results in lower income and output for the economy as a whole because labor is not allowed to seek its most productive employment.[21] This assertion can be demonstrated by means of a model incorporating relatively simple and straightforward assumptions.

Assume an economy which is characterized by the ultimate in overcrowding. Only two occupations exist, with all the labor in one occupation being male (N_M) and all the labor in the other occupation being female (N_F). N_M and N_F are assumed to be perfect substitutes for each other. The size of the male labor force is given by N_M, while the size of the female labor force is given by N_F. The total labor force is the sum of N_M and N_F.

The production function for the economy is given by

$$Q = f(N_M, N_F, K) \tag{3.11}$$

where K = units of capital

The explicit production function is a modified C.E.S. form:

$$Q^{-\beta} = a_1 N_M^{-\beta} + a_2 N_F^{-\beta} + a_3 K^{-\beta} \tag{3.12}$$

where β = a parameter depending upon the elasticity of substitution between factor inputs

a_i = parameter reflecting overcrowding or underrepresentation

The marginal products of male and female labor are signified by MP_M and MP_F, respectively, and are equal to

$$MP_M = a_1 (Q/N_N)^{\beta+1} \tag{3.13}$$

$$MP_F = a_2 (Q/N_F)^{\beta+1} \tag{3.14}$$

In the absence of sex discrimination, male and female labor move freely among occupations and equate MP_M and MP_F. Let E_M^* and E_F^* represent the employment of male and female labor, respectively, after all desired movement in labor between occupations has occurred. The equality-of-marginal-products rule requires that Equation (3.15) hold:

$$a_1 (Q/E_M^*)^{\beta+1} = a_2 (Q/E_F^*)^{\beta+1} \tag{3.15}$$

If, following the tradition of Bergmann, N_M and N_F are assumed to be infinitely inelastic in supply, then it follows that

$$E_F^* = N_M + N_F - E_M^* \qquad (3.16)$$

Substituting Equation (3.16) into equation (3.15) yields

$$E_M^* = \frac{a_1^\sigma}{a_1^\sigma + a_2^\sigma} (N_M + N_F) \qquad (3.17)$$

where $\sigma = 1/(1 + \beta)$ and is the elasticity of substitution between N_M and N_F

Similar manipulation yields

$$E_F^* = \frac{a_2^\sigma}{a_1^\sigma + a_2^\sigma} (N_M + N_F) \qquad (3.18)$$

The cost of sex discrimination can be represented by the difference between output before and after sex discrimination. Let Q represent output before sex discrimination and Q^* represent output after sex discrimination. From Equations (3.13) and (3.14), we know that

$$\frac{MP_M^*}{MP_M} = (Q^*/Q)^{\beta+1} (N_M/E_M^*)^{\beta+1} \qquad (3.19)$$

Hence, the ratio of postdiscrimination output to prediscrimination output is given by

$$Q^*/Q = \frac{(MP^*/MP)^{1/(\beta+1)}}{(N_M/E_M^*)} \qquad (3.20)$$

The expectation is that Q^*/Q in Equation (3.20) will be less than 1.00 due to sex discrimination. Bergmann found, however, that the ratio Q^*/Q was only slightly less than 1.00 in the case of racial discrimination, even under the most favorable assumptions. Hence, the total loss in productivity because of discrimination may not be large. On the other hand, Bergmann also found that the elimination of racial discrimination would result in ". . . very considerable gains . . . by Negroes . . . at the expense of trivial losses for most white males and moderate losses for virtually all other white males."[22] Thus, to the extent that one can extrapolate from racial discrimination to sexual discrimination, empirical evidence relating to the overcrowding hypothesis suggests that the distributional consequences of overcrowding are quantitatively far more important than the economywide productivity consequences. The elimination of sex discrimination due to overcrowding would, if one follows this chain of reasoning, bring substantial gains to female employees, but minimal gains to the economy as a whole.

The Marxian View of Discrimination

The Marxian theory of discrimination is intimately related to Marx's views concerning "exploitation."[23] Marx argued that workers produce output which has substantially more value than the expense of supporting and replacing these same workers. Specifically, the wage a worker is paid is less than the value of the output that the worker produces. The difference is exploitation. In the Marxian scheme of things, exploitation occurs when payments are made to factors of production other than labor. Payments to capital, for example, are unnecessary because capital is nothing more than dead labor.

Marxian exploitation is actually the value of output (after all worn-out factor inputs have been replaced) minus the cost of supporting workers at a subsistence level of consumption. Only when entire value of the output produced (after the worn-out factor inputs have been replaced) goes to labor for purposes of current consumption does exploitation disappear.

When Marxian exploitation is absent, there is no net investment. This follows from the fact that any *additions* to the capital stock are, by matter of definition, exploitation. Note also that Marxian exploitation does not occur because of the presence of monopoly or monopsony power. Even it perfect competition existed, there would still be Marxian exploitation. The payment to labor of the value of labor's marginal product represents Marxian exploitation. In order to avoid Marxian exploitation, workers must receive all the value of output not devoted to replacing worn-out factor inputs.

Marxian exploitation assumes that factors of production other than labor will continue to be supplied to the productive process even when these factor inputs are not paid a positive supply price. Marx ignores the opportunity cost of factor inputs such as capital and land. Their alternative uses in an economic context are assumed away.

The connection of Marxian exploitation to discrimination is simply that capitalists find it easier to exploit certain workers than others. Capitalist institutions such as slavery, marriage, and the family make it easy for race and sex discrimination to occur. Engles, for example, devoted an entire book to propounding the thesis that marriage and the family are capitalist institutions designed to exploit women and preserve male economic hegemony.[24]

August Bebel, a more recent Marxian writer, saw the entrance of women into the labor force as a logical extension of the Marxian concept of the "industiral reserve army of the unemployed."[25] In this view, a massive legion of unemployed workers competing for scarce jobs would drive wages down to the subsistence level and guarantee exploitation. Bebel looked upon women as wage reducers. Capitalists would use female participation in the labor force as a means to bid the total wages going to a family down to the subsistence level. Women, then, are industrial helots who are exploited by capitalists. They are exploited because of the inherent nature of capitalism, which seeks out the most available victims. Capitalism and sex discrimination walk hand in hand.

Summary

The original Becker model of discrimination assumed perfect competition and constant returns to scale. Discrimination could take place, but only at a cost to the discriminator, who would suffer a loss in output. By way of contrast, monopsony models of discrimination typically predict that the discriminator can gain by discriminating. Discriminating monopsony is possible when the discriminating firm has monopsony power and can segment the labor market, and when the segments of the labor have differing wage elasticities of supply.

A variant of the discriminating monopsony model is the overcrowding hypothesis. In this view, disproportionate numbers of female workers are forced to work in certain industries, thus driving down their marginal productivities in that industry and therefore their wages. Whether overcrowding increases the total share of income going to female labor depends upon the elasticity of substitution between male and female labor. Whether overcrowding increases the total wage payment made to labor depends upon the wage elasticity of demand for female labor.

Marxist theory views discrimination as an inevitable outcome of capitalist production. Capitalist institutions such as marriage and the family force female labor to be part of the reserve army of the unemployed. All workers in capitalism are exploited; this exploitation falls differentially hard upon females because capitalist institutions make females most vulnerable to discrimination and exploitation.

4

A Review of Empirical Studies of Sex Discrimination and Affirmative Action

"The cause of lightning," Alice said very decidedly, for she felt quite sure about this, "is the thunder—no, no!" she hastily corrected herself, "I meant the other way."

"It's too late to correct it," said the Red Queen: "When you've once said a thing, that fixes it, and you must take the consequences."

Empirical studies which purport to describe the incidence and amount of sex discrimination of the economy have become relatively common. Unfortunately, only a minority of these studies are reliable in terms of the data set involved, the specification of the crucial variables, and statistical technique utilized. Indeed, most of the casual empiricism which characterizes sex discrimination judgments is grossly inadequate on some of or all the above counts.

An important example of the problems associated with much of the current empirical work dealing with sex discrimination is the salary kit developed by Bergmann and Maxfield.[1] This salary kit has at least the implicit approval of the American Association of University Professors (AAUP), and it purports to be a method by which someone might evaluate the "fairness" of a faculty salary structure with respect to sex. The University of Maryland was used as an example. Bergmann and Maxfield estimated a linear regression equation in an attempt to discover the determinants of male faculty salaries at the University of Maryland. Then, using the regression coefficients from this equation, they generated a counterfactual estimate of what women faculty at the University of Maryland would have been paid had they been paid on the same basis as male faculty. This resulted in the judgment that the actual salaries of the 166 female faculty in the sample were $275,604 per year less than their counterfactual salary. This was an average of $1,660 per female faculty member.[2]

The primary problem with the Bergmann-Maxfield salary kit is not the counterfactual methodology, since counterfactualism coincides neatly with the equal-pay-for-equal-work requirements of the law. Rather, Bergmann and Maxfield omitted from their predictive equation any measures of faculty productivity and performance. Academic rank was omitted from the equation

Lewis Carroll, *Through the Looking Glass*, in *The Philosopher's Alice* (New York: St. Martin's Press, 1974), p. 228.

43

specification on the ground that it was susceptible to sex discrimination. The only variable which even remotely measured individual faculty productivity and performance was the number of years that had passed since the faculty member had obtained his or her degree.

It is impossible to make a reliable judgment about equal pay for equal work if there is no consideration given to interfaculty variations in productivity and performance. To say that equal pay for equal work is or is not being satisfied without looking at the amount and quality of work performed is to so seriously bias an analysis that it is of doubtful use. In defense of Bergmann and Maxfield, they did acknowledge that differential faculty productivity might account for some of the observed differences in faculty salaries between the sexes. However, the mere citing of such a caveat does not absolve Bergmann and Maxfield of the misapplications and misinterpretations of their model which will result because the model lacks productivity and performance information for individual faculty. This is particularly true when the apparent imprimatur of the AAUP is stamped upon the salary kit.

The misspecification of the Bergmann-Maxfield model has sex implications for faculty salaries. However, it additionally has profound implications for the distribution of salaries among female faculty members. A salary kit which equates years with productivity is biased in favor of older, less productive faculty. It is biased against younger faculty and particularly is injurious to those younger faculty who produce extensive scholarship of high quality. The Bergmann-Maxfield salary kit distorts which female faculty members are said to be underpaid relative to their male counterparts. This may be inequitable, and it is clearly uneconomic.

The Bergmann-Maxfield effort is, all things considered, a more solidly founded study than most others. A typical statement concerning sex discrimination in faculty salaries will cite the absolute difference between male and female salaries as being the result of discrimination. While this may be true, the conclusion does not follow logically since male and female faculty differ in terms of degree status, experience, departmental identity, prestige of school where employed, as well as productivity and performance. An example in point is the citation in *Women Today* of the fact that in the 1974-75 academic year, the mean salary of male faculty in the United States was $15,926, while the mean salary of female faculty was $13,243.[3] The relevant point is that it is impossible to tell from this data whether sex discrimination is present.

Our strategy in evaluating the available empirical studies relating to sex discrimination and affirmative action will be initially to look at economywide data concerning sex discrimination in jobs and wages. We will then analyze the overall wage situation in academia. This will be followed by a review of studies of sex discrimination and affirmative action in particular universities and in particular disciplines. Finally, we will critically examine the limited evidence available that bears on possible sex differences in labor force participation rates, quit rates, expected future productivity, and peer evaluation of performance.

Economywide Evidence Relating to Sex Discrimination

In the area of employment, women have been concentrated disproportionately in certain occupations. Table 4-1 reveals that in the year 1964 only 6 percent of the total number of employees in mining were women, whereas 82 percent of the total number of employees in hospitals were women. Table 4-1 also reveals, however, that the sex composition of employment in some industries has been changing slowly. For example, between the years 1964 and 1973, the amount of women employed in educational services rose from 44 to 49 percent, while the amount of women employed in telephone communications fell from 56 to 51 percent.

Some of the most notable changes in the employment situation of women have occurred in the skilled trades. Table 4-2 indicates that, for example, the amount of women employed as furniture and wood finishers rose from 3.5 percent in 1960 to 16.9 percent in 1970. In general, the representation of women in the skilled trades increased dramatically over this time period.

What interpretation can we place upon the data contained in Table 4-1 and 4-2? Clearly, women employees have tended to be relegated to certain occupations and excluded or discouraged from others. Yet, in the absence of detailed information about education and skill requirements for various occupations and the actual desired labor force choices of both men and women employees, it is difficult to make a precise estimate concerning the precise amount of employment discrimination that has taken place. Suffice it to say that there is general agreement that women are underrepresented in many occupations, and overrepresented in other occupations, relative to their qualifications, the requirements of those jobs, and their labor force characteristics.

The actual earnings of women employees also imply the existence of sex discrimination. Table 4-3 contains information relating to the hourly earnings of men and women employees in a wide range of educational and demographic categories. In 1959, the ratio of the hourly earnings of women to the hourly earnings of men (for white, nonfarm employees) was only 0.61. This proportion rose to 0.64 in 1969. The differential between the hourly earnings of men and women is less obvious in governmental employment. It is generally greatest in the lowest educational categories.

Once again, what interpretation should we place upon the data contained in Table 4-3? One can easily infer broad evidence of sex discrimination from the information found there. Nonetheless, the data in Table 4-3 are not controlled for possible sex differences in labor force participation rates, quit rates, and expected future productivity. On the other hand, it is doubtful, even should such

Table 4-1
Women Employees on Nonagricultural Payrolls, by Selected Industries January 1964 and January 1973 (Numbers in Thousands)

Industry Group	1964		1973	
	Number of Women	Percent of Total Employed	Number of Women	Percent of Total Employed
Total nonagricultural industries	19,096	34	27,920	38
Private	15,421	33	21,854	37
Mining	34	6	37	6
Construction	143	6	193	6
Manufacturing	4,385	26	5,464	28
Durable goods	1,717	18	2,357	21
Fabricated metal products	192	17	264	19
Machinery, except electrical	201	13	297	15
Electrical equipment and supplies	571	37	781	41
Transportation equipment	168	10	199	11
Instruments and related products	123	34	183	38
Miscellaneous manufacturing	145	40	179	43
Nondurable goods	2,668	37	3,107	39
Food and kindred products	387	23	420	25
Meat products	79	25	94	28
Poultry dressing plants	35	53	52	55
Canned, cured, and frozen foods	85	42	89	39
Canned, cured, and frozen seafoods	20	58	21	56
Confectionary and related products	39	51	41	51
Tobacco manufacturers	40	46	30	42
Textile mill products	373	43	467	46
Knitting mills	134	67	174	65
Apparel and other textile products	994	79	1,062	81

Table 4–1 (Continued)
Women Employees on Nonagricultural Payrolls, by Selected Industries 1964 and January 1973
(Numbers in Thousands)

Industry Group	1964		1973	
	Number of Women	Percent of Total Employed	Number of Women	Percent of Total Employed
Printing and publishing	270	29	366	34
Periodicals	33	48	34	50
Blankbooks and bookbinding	21	45	29	51
Chemicals and allied products	160	19	208	21
Leather and leather products	179	53	175	60
Transportation and public utilities	706	18	949	21
Communications	410	50	542	47
Telephone communication	380	56	493	51
Radio and television broadcasting	22	22	34	25
Wholesale and retail trade	4,404	37	6,338	40
Wholesale trade	686	22	912	23
Retail trade	3,718	43	5,426	46
Retail general merchandise	1,163	70	1,708	68
Food stores	451	32	694	37
Apparel and accessory stores	387	65	505	66
Eating and drinking places	969	56	1,431	55
Miscellaneous retail stores	427	42	620	46
Drug stores and proprietary stores	222	58	295	62
Finance, insurance, and real estate	1,445	50	2,070	52
Banking	454	60	721	64
Credit agencies other than banks	167	54	234	57
Security, commodity brokers, and services	38	31	68	35
Insurance carriers	435	49	578	52
Insurance agents, brokers, and service	124	56	172	59
Real estate	190	36	250	34

Table 4–1 (Continued)
Women Employees on Nonagricultural Payrolls, by Selected Industries 1964 and January 1973
(Numbers in Thousands)

Industry Group	1964		1973	
	Number of Women	Percent of Total Employed	Number of Women	Percent of Total Employed
Services	4,304	51	6,803	55
Hotels, tourist courts, and motels	245	48	346	52
Personal services	553	60	555	62
Miscellaneous business services	333	34	600	35
Advertising	40	37	50	43
Credit reporting and collection	43	70	57	71
Services to buildings	42	27	119	35
Medical and other health services	1,474	78	2,850	80
Hospitals	1,029	82	1,641	80
Legal services	105	62	171	63
Educational services	398	44	593	49
Elementary and secondary schools	175	58	255	61
Colleges and universities	197	37	272	42
Government	3,675	39	6,066	45
Federal	520	22	767	29
State	692	38	1,248	43
State education	245	40	535	43
Other state government	448	37	713	43
Local	2,463	46	4,050	50
Local education	1,831	63	2,956	63
Other local government	633	26	1,095	32

Note: Because some industries are not included in this table, subgroups do not always add to the total for major industrial division.

Source: Reprinted with permission from the *Monthly Labor Review*, 97 (May 1974), p. 6.

Table 4-2
Women Employed in the Skilled Trades, by Detailed Trade, 1960 and 1970

Trade[a]	Number of Women Employed			Women as Percent of Total	
	1960[b]	1970	Change, 1960-70	1960	1970
Total	277,140	494,871	217,731	3.1	5.0
Automobile accessories installers	—	297	297	—	4.4
Bakers	20,283	32,665	12,382	18.0	29.8
Blacksmiths	101	249	148	0.5	2.4
Blue-collar worker supervisor, n.e.c.	77,728	127,751	50,023	7.2	8.0
Construction	206	1,608	1,402	0.2	1.1
Durable manufacturing	14,724	25,539	10,815	4.1	4.6
Nondurable manufacturing, including not specified	40,882	52,193	11,311	13.9	14.4
Transportation, communications, and other public utilities	2,480	5,676	3,196	1.2	3.7
All other industries	19,436	42,735	23,299	9.1	11.8
Boilermakers	41	371	330	0.2	1.3
Bookbinders	16,513	19,461	2,948	57.9	57.1
Brickmasons and stonemasons	722	2,049	1,327	0.5	1.3
Bulldozer operators	—	1,151	1,151	—	1.3
Cabinetmakers	891	3,429	2,538	1.3	5.1
Carpenters	3,312	11,059	7,747	0.4	1.3
Carpet installers	—	754	754	—	1.7
Cement and concrete finishers	100	908	808	0.2	1.4
Compositors and typesetters	15,494	23,962	8,468	8.2	15.0
Crane, derrick, and hoist operators	656	1,952	1,296	0.5	1.3
Decorators and window dressers	23,566	40,408	16,852	46.3	57.6
Dental laboratory technicians	641	6,057	5,416	4.3	22.7

Table 4-2 (continued)
Women Employed in the Skilled Trades, by Detailed Trade, 1960 and 1970

Trade[a]	Number of Women Employed			Women as Percent of Total	
	1960[b]	1970	Change, 1960-70	1960	1970
Electricians	2,483	8,646	6,163	0.7	1.8
Electric power and cable installers	1,648	1,457	−191	2.1	1.4
Electrotypers and stereotypers	72	283	211	0.8	4.0
Engravers, except photoengravers	1,948	2,333	385	17.3	26.6
Excavating, grading, road machine operators except bulldozer operators	688	2,513	1,825	0.4	1.1
Floor layers, except tile setters	882	364	−518	4.9	1.7
Forge and hammer operators	769	724	−45	6.4	4.7
Furniture and wood finishers	768	3,600	2,832	3.5	16.9
Furriers	1,936	461	−1,475[c]	40.4	17.3
Glaziers	227	783	556	1.3	3.1
Heat treaters, annealers, and temperers	293	598	305	1.4	2.9
Inspectors, scalers, and graders, log and lumber	798	1,877	1,079	3.9	11.0
Inspectors, n.e.c.	5,670	8,865	3,195	5.8	7.5
Construction	100	334	234	0.7	1.5
Railroads and railway express service	76	247	171	0.3	1.0
Jewelers and watchmakers	2,239	4,285	2,046	6.0	11.5
Job and die setters, metal	322	2,221	1,899	0.6	2.6
Locomotive engineers	85	396	311	0.1	0.8
Locomotive fire fighters	104	151	47	0.3	1.2
Machinists	6,685	11,787	5,102	1.3	3.1
Mechanics and repairers	18,329	49,349	31,020	0.9	2.0
Air conditioning, heating, and refrigeration	125	1,065	940	0.2	0.9
Aircraft	1,668	4,013	2,345	1.5	2.9

Table 4-2 (continued)
Women Employed in the Skilled Trades, by Detailed Trade, 1960 and 1970

Trade[a]	Number of Women Employed			Women as Percent of Total	
	1960[b]	1970	Change, 1960-70	1960	1970
Automobile body repairers	—	1,332	1,332	—	1.2
Automobile mechanics	2,270	11,130	8,860	0.4	1.4
Data processing machine repairers	—	864	864	—	2.7
Farm implement	—	420	420	—	1.2
Heavy equipment mechanics, including diesel	3,345	10,768	7,423	1.2	1.8
Household appliance and accessory installers and mechanics	—	2,550	2,550	—	2.1
Loom fixers	208	437	229	0.9	2.1
Office machine	279	688	409	0.9	1.2
Radio and television	1,688	5,032	3,344	1.7	3.7
Railroad and car shop	332	510	178	0.6	0.9
Other	8,414	10,540	2,126	1.2	4.2
Millers, grain, flour, and feed	64	161	97	0.7	2.3
Millwrights	80	903	823	0.7	1.2
Molders, metal	1,452	5,757	4,305	2.9	0.6
Motion picture projectionists	390	670	280	2.2	4.2
Opticians and lens grinders and polishers	3,045	6,121	3,076	15.0	2.3
Painters, construction and maintenance	6,449	13,386	6,937	1.9	4.1
Paperhangers	1,455	1,111	-344[c]	6.0	10.8
Pattern and model makers, except paper	647	1,858	1,211	1.6	4.8
Photoengravers and lithographers	2,847	3,851	1,004	10.4	11.8
Piano and organ tuners and repairers	153	330	177	2.5	4.8
Plasterers	158	435	277	0.3	1.5
Plumbers and pipe fitters	952	4,110	3,158	0.3	1.1
Power station operators	1,375	557	-818[c]	5.1	3.0
Printing press operators	4,848	13,374	8,526	5.8	8.5

Table 4-2 (continued)
Women Employed in the Skilled Trades, by Detailed Trade, 1960 and 1970

Trade[a]	Number of Women Employed			Women as Percent of Total	
	1960[b]	1970	Change, 1960-70	1960	1970
Rollers and finishers, metal	802	1,264	462	4.2	6.4
Roffers and slaters	107	749	642	0.2	1.3
Sheetmetal workers and tinsmiths	1,530	2,902	1,372	1.1	1.9
Shipfitters	–	123	123	–	1.2
Shoe repairers	2,759	6,359	3,600	6.7	20.3
Sign painters and letterers	1,286	1,614	328	4.6	8.5
Stationary engineers	1,563	2,472	909	0.5	1.4
Stone cutters and stone carvers	132	445	313	2.0	2.0
Structural metal workers	909	883	– 26	1.5	1.2
Tailors	21,728	21,265	– 463[c]	26.5	31.4
Telephone installers and repairers	3,018	8,289	5,271	2.0	3.5
Telephone line installers and repairers	824	762	– 62	2.0	1.5
Tile setters	–	378	378	–	1.2
Tool and die makers	1,128	4,197	3,069	0.6	2.1
Upholsterers	5,668	9,980	4,312	9.4	16.0
Craft and kindred workers, n.e.c.	5,777	7,339	1,562	6.7	8.5

[a]Some of the occupational titles that appear in this table and elsewhere in the article are recent modifications of older titles which denoted or connoted sex stereotyping. The new titles were accomplished by a subcommittee of the Interagency Committee on Occupational Classification, under the auspices of the Office of Management and Budget. (See "Removal of Sex Stereotyping in Census Occupational Classification," *Monthly Labor Review*, January 1974, pp. 67-68.)

[b]Adjusted to 1970 occupation classifications. See John A. Priebe, Joan Heninkel, and Stanley Green, "1970 Occupation and Industry Classification Systems in terms of their 1960 Occupation and Industry Elements," Technical Paper 26 (Bureau of the Census, 1972).

[c]Also showed a decline in total employment.

Note: Data was taken from the 1970 Census.

Source: Reprinted with permission from the *Monthly Labor Review*, 97 (May 1974), p. 16.

Table 4-3
Hourly Earnings of White Non-Farm-Employed Men and Women, 1959 and 1969

Characteristic	Average Hourly Earnings, 1969		Ratio of Hourly Earnings of Women and Men[a]		
	Women	Men	1959	1969	Percent Change, 1959-69
All	$2.70	$4.46	0.61	0.64	4.8
Northeast	2.92	4.71	0.63	0.66	5.2
North Central	2.68	4.52	0.61	0.62	2.2
South	2.41	3.98	0.60	0.63	5.8
West	2.89	4.78	0.60	0.64	6.4
12 years of schooling or less	2.41	3.84	0.61	0.62	1.5
More than 12 years of schooling	3.44	5.75	0.59	0.66	11.4
Less than 35 years of age	2.64	4.19	0.71	0.74	3.1
35 years of age or more	2.79	4.84	0.57	0.59	4.2
Married, spouse present	2.69	4.67	0.59	0.61	3.0
Never married	2.72	3.06	0.81	0.86	6.0
Other	2.71	4.04	0.65	0.69	6.0
Less than 35 years of age:					
Married, spouse present	2.64	4.46	0.73	0.70	-3.4
Never married	2.59	2.90	0.81	0.86	6.1
Other	2.73	3.87	0.71	0.80	13.0
35 years of age or more:					
Married, spouse present	2.76	4.94	0.56	0.57	3.0
Never married	3.25	3.86	0.78	0.80	2.9
Other	2.69	4.22	0.64	0.67	4.5
Private wage and salary workers	2.52	4.27	0.59	0.62	5.2
Government workers	3.43	4.44	0.79	0.77	-2.4
Self-employed workers	2.71	5.68	0.51	0.57	11.4
Less than 35 years of age:					
Private wage and salary workers	2.48	4.02	0.71	0.73	2.2
Government workers	3.29	4.26	0.82	0.84	3.2
Self-employed workers	2.74	5.51	0.73	0.69	-5.4
35 years of age or more:					
Private wage and salary workers	2.59	4.68	0.54	0.57	5.1
Government workers	3.64	4.66	0.76	0.72	-5.4
Self-employed workers	2.69	5.81	0.50	0.57	13.9

[a]The female-male earnings ratio (R) adjusted for age and schooling is calculated in the following way:

$$R = (F/\hat{F} + \hat{M}/M)/2$$

where F = average hourly earnings of females

Table 4-3 (Cont.)

M = average hourly earnings of males
H = total annual hours worked by females
K = total annual hours worked by males
subscripts a and s = age group a and schooling group s,

$$\hat{F} = \sum_{as} (M_{as} H_{as})/\sum_{as} H_{as} \quad \text{and} \quad \hat{M} = \sum_{as} (F_{as} K_{as})/\sum_{as} K_{as}$$

It is, therefore, an average of the results obtained by standardizing hours worked by women on wage rates of men, and hours worked by men on wage rates of women, across 49 age-schooling cells. The percentage change in the ratio from 1959 to 1969 is (100) $(R_{70} - R_{60})/R_{60}$ (calculated from unrounded data).

Note: Because of limitations of time and space, the focus of this discussion is on the sex differential in earnings for white workers only. It is noteworthy, however, that the differential in earnings between black men and black women narrowed appreciably from 1959 to 1969, as did the differential between blacks and whites. During the decade, earnings of black women, adjusted for age and schooling, rose 82 percent compared with 68 percent for black men and 53 percent for white women. By 1959, less than 15 percent separated the earnings of black women and white women of comparable age and schooling. For women with more than 12 years of schooling, the adjusted differential between blacks and whites had practically disappeared.

Source: Reprinted with permission from the *Monthly Labor Review*, 97 (May 1974), p. 24.

differentials exist, that they could explain the entirety of the earnings differentials observed in Table 4-3. The relevant point, however, with respect to Tables 4-1 through 4-3, is that such aggregated data make it very difficult to judge whether economic sex discrimination is present. In the case of a particular employee, it is virtually impossible to make any sort of judgment about discrimination based upon the data presented in these tables.

Rigorous studies of sex discrimination at the economywide level have typically examined the wage differential between male and female employees in particular occupations. A wide variety of results have been reported. At one extreme, Sanborn found a 12 percent differential between male and female earnings when he utilized a subsample of the civilian labor force for the year 1950.[4] He controlled for occupation, hours worked, age, education, race, location, turnover, absenteeism, and experience. At the other extreme, Sawhill has estimated that the differential is about 43 percent, with a major portion of the differential due to a Bergmann type of overcrowding in certain occupations.[5] Other reliable studies, each with a varying methodology and data set, have produced intermediate estimates of the earnings differential, for example, Morgan-Cohen-David-Brazer (37 percent),[6] Fuchs (34 percent),[7] Cohen (31 percent),[8] Oaxaca (29 percent),[9] and Suter-Miller (31 percent).[10]

Earnings differentials between men and women do exist, and while a substantial portion of the observed differentials may be explained by means of sex differences in labor force participation, quit rates, and productivity,[11] an unexplained residual remains that is ordinarily imputed to discrimination. Further, it may be the case that peer evaluations and reactions to female performance are biased downward relative to that of males. That is, the same performance by a male and a female results in a lower evaluation for the female. If so, then the earnings differentials are underestimated, at least with respect to this factor.

In general, the more homogeneous the labor market, and the more micro the data set, the more we can say about the presence or absence of discrimination. For that reason, we will now turn to the empirical evidence that has accumulated relating to sex discrimination in academia.

Evidence Relating to Sex Discrimination in Academia at Large

The most reputable source of aggregative data about faculty salaries is the annual survey of faculty salaries and compensation carried out by the American Association of University Professors (AAUP). Nearly all institutions of higher education of any note participate in the AAUP survey, which traditionally has been published in the summer issue of the *AAUP Bulletin*.[12] The annual survey addresses itself to tenure status and academic rank by sex in addition to report salaries and compensation.

Table 4-4 reveals that fewer female academics have achieved tenure than male academics. In category I (primarily Ph.D.-granting institutions), only 42 percent of women faculty have achieved tenure, whereas the comparable datum for men is 66 percent. The relative position of women faculty vis-à-vis tenure improves somewhat in the non-Ph.D.-granting institutions, the small four-year colleges, and the two-year colleges (categories IIA, IIB, and III in Table 4-4).

The average salary of a female full professor at a category I institution was 10.2 percent lower than that for a male full professor in the 1974-75 academic year, according to Table 4-5. Once again, this differential lessens in the less comprehensive, generally less prestigious institutions. For example, the same differential is only 3.1 percent in category III (two-year) institutions. Table 4-6 reports similar information in terms of absolute dollars for women, while Table 4-7 does the same for men. Consistent with the results of Table 4-5, we find in Table 4-6 that the mean salary of a female full professor at a category I institution was $20,650 in the 1974-75 academic year, while the comparable datum for a male full professor was $22,990.

The crucial question with respect to the salary differentials which appear in Table 4-5 through 4-7 is whether this is evidence of sex discrimination. The answer is that such differentials may be the result of sex discrimination against female faculty; however, it is impossible to determine the extent to which that is true, given the data. Other than academic rank, there is no control for possible differential performance and productivity between male and female faculty. Similarly, the AAUP data are not controlled for possible sex differences in labor force participation and quit rates, or for possible discrimination in peer

Table 4-4
Percentage of Full-time Faculty Members with Tenure Status, by Category, Type of Affiliation, Academic Rank, and Sex

Academic Rank	Total				Men				Women			
	All Combined	Public	Private Independent	Church Related	All Combined	Public	Private Independent	Church Related	All Combined	Public	Private Independent	Church Related
Category I												
Professor	96%	96%	97%	95%	97%	97%	98%	95%	95%	94%	95%	96%
Associate	83	85	70	83	83	86	70	82	81	83	71	85
Assistant	18	20	5	20	16	18	5	19	25	27	8	25
Instructor	7	8	1	4	6	7	1	2	8	9	2	5
All ranks	62	63	59	58	66	67	63	62	42	43	33	41
Category IIA												
Professor	94	94	95	92	94	94	96	93	94	95	93	88
Associate	80	81	78	78	80	81	77	78	81	82	80	74
Assistant	37	40	25	28	35	38	25	27	41	45	25	31
Instructor	14	18	4	4	13	16	5	4	15.	19	3	3
All ranks	61	63	55	55	64	66	59	59	51	54	40	39
Category IIB												
Professor	94	88	95	95	94	88	95	95	91	89	94	90
Associate	77	76	78	77	77	76	78	78	75	74	77	74
Assistant	27	31	19	30	25	27	19	28	32	40	19	35
Instructor	6	8	9	3	6	8	8	2	6	8	9	3
All ranks	53	48	52	57	57	51	55	61	41	40	40	43

Table 4-4 (continued)
Percentage of Full-time Faculty Members with Tenure Status, by Category, Type of Affiliation, Academic Rank, and Sex

Academic Rank	Total				Men				Women			
	All Combined	Public	Private Independent	Church Related	All Combined	Public	Private Independent	Church Related	All Combined	Public	Private Independent	Church Related
Category III												
Professor	92	92	100	83	90	90	—	83	96	96	—	80
Associate	82	82	92	61	81	81	93	63	84	84	92	56
Assistant	49	50	28	31	51	52	28	38	46	47	27	20
Instructor	17	17	15	13	21	21	15	39	13	13	15	6
All ranks	53	54	39	33	57	58	40	42	44	45	38	20
Category IV												
No rank	64	66	31	41	67	69	32	41	59	61	27	40
All Categories except IV												
Professor	95	95	96	94	95	95	97	94	94	94	94	90
Associate	81	83	75	78	81	83	74	79	80	82	77	75
Assistant	29	32	15	28	27	29	15	26	34	38	17	32
Instructor	11	13	5	3	11	13	5	3	11	13	5	3
All ranks	60	62	56	56	64	67	60	60	46	48	38	41

Note: Sample includes 1,189 institutions providing data on tenure status (134 category I, 363 category IIa, 422 category IIB, 103 category III, and 167 category IV institutions). Category I institutions offer the doctorate and in the last three years conferred a mean of at least 15 doctorates per year in three or more nonrelated disciplines. Category IIA institutions award degrees above the baccalaureate, but are not included in category I. Category IIB institutions award only the baccalaureate degree. Category III institutions are two-year in nature. Category IV institutions include colleges and universities without academic ranks.

Source: Reprinted with permission from the *AAUP Bulletin*, 61 (Summer 1975), Table 24, p. 139.

Table 4-5
Percentage Differences between the Average Salaries and Average Compensation of Men and Women Faculty Members, by Category, Type of Affiliation, and Academic Rank, 1974-75[a]

Academic Rank	Salary				Compensation			
	All Combined	Public	Private Independent	Church Related	All Combined	Public	Private Independent	Church Related
Category I								
Professor	10.2%	9.5%	12.1%	9.0%	10.5%	9.5%	12.7%	9.0%
Associate	4.7	4.5	4.5	7.3	4.7	4.5	4.5	7.0
Assistant	5.4	5.6	4.3	5.7	5.4	5.3	4.5	5.6
Instructor	4.8	5.4	-0.9	6.0	5.0	5.6	-1.8	6.3
All ranks	22.3	19.3	24.1	19.6	22.4	21.9	24.5	19.4
Average within-rank difference[b]	5.7	5.8	5.0	6.5	5.8	5.7	5.1	6.4
Category IIA								
Professor	3.0	2.7	6.6	10.3	3.1	2.6	6.7	11.0
Associate	1.9	-0.9	4.4	8.7	1.9	0.9	4.3	9.7
Assistant	3.1	2.6	5.0	7.1	3.0	2.4	4.8	7.5
Instructor	4.3	4.0	5.1	4.3	4.6	4.3	5.8	5.0
All ranks	13.0	12.3	15.2	17.7	13.0	12.3	15.4	18.4
Average within-rank difference[b]	3.1	2.1	5.1	7.1	3.1	2.5	5.2	7.7
Category IIB								
Professor	6.1	6.0	3.5	8.5	7.1	6.6	2.8	10.2
Associate	6.3	4.5	3.9	6.8	6.8	4.5	3.7	7.9
Assistant	5.0	4.7	4.0	5.6	5.3	5.1	3.6	6.1
Instructor	4.9	4.1	4.7	4.9	5.1	4.1	4.8	5.6
All ranks	13.8	12.7	13.3	14.3	14.3	12.9	13.1	15.4
Average within-rank difference[b]	5.4	4.6	4.0	6.1	5.8	4.8	3.7	6.9

Table 4-5 (continued)

Percentage Differences between the Average Salaries and Average Compensation of Men and Women Faculty Members, by Category, Type of Affiliation, and Academic Rank, 1974-75[a]

Academic Rank	Salary				Compensation			
	All Combined	Public	Private Independent	Church Related	All Combined	Public	Private Independent	Church Related
				Category III				
Professor	3.1	2.3	—	—	3.5	2.7	—	—
Associate	1.2	0.1	6.9	6.0	1.2	0.1	7.4	6.2
Assistant	0.7	0.5	3.9	1.1	0.7	0.4	5.8	1.7
Instructor	4.6	3.9	0.8	0.8	4.4	3.5	1.1	1.2
All ranks	8.5	7.9	7.5	6.9	8.5	7.8	8.7	7.9
Average within-rank difference[b]	2.2	1.7	2.9	1.6	2.2	2.7	3.5	2.1
				Category IV				
No rank	9.0	8.8	5.8	3.7	9.1	8.8	7.6	4.5
			All Categories Combined Except IV					
Professor	9.2	6.5	13.4	11.1	8.4	6.5	13.7	12.0
Associate	3.8	1.8	6.3	8.6	3.8	2.1	6.2	9.4
Assistant	3.8	3.4	5.0	6.3	3.7	3.1	4.9	6.7
Instructor	4.5	4.4	4.7	4.7	4.7	4.5	4.7	5.2
All ranks	17.4	16.5	21.6	27.4	17.5	16.4	21.9	17.9
Average within-rank difference[b]	4.6	3.7	6.6	6.9	4.5	3.6	6.5	7.5

[a]Sample includes 1,351 institutions submitting data broken down by sex.

[b]Average of percent differences for the ranks, weighted by proportion of women in rank.

Note: A negative sign indicates that women are paid more than men. Category definitions may be found at the bottom of Table 4-4. Dashes indicate that the sample was too small to be meaningful.

Source: Reprinted with permission from the *AAUP Bulletin*, 61 (Summer 1975), Table 21, p. 137.

Table 4-6
Weighted Average Salaries and Average Compensations for Women Faculty Members, by Category, Type of Affiliation, and Academic Rank, 1974-75

Academic Rank	Salary				Compensation			
	All Combined	Public	Private Independent	Church Related	All Combined	Public	Private Independent	Church Related
Category I								
Professor	$20,650	$20,600	$21,690	$19,020	$23,330	$23,150	$25,190	$21,550
Associate	16,110	16,130	16,490	15,040	18,250	18,220	19,070	17,210
Assistant	13,190	13,220	13,280	12,620	15,010	15,040	15,200	14,420
Instructor	10,530	10,480	11,070	10,450	11,950	11,910	12,490	11,830
All ranks[a]	14,060	14,030	14,650	13,370	15,920	15,830	16,920	15,250
Category IIA								
Professor	20,660	21,100	19,190	16,410	23,360	23,790	22,330	18,730
Associate	16,380	16,790	15,400	13,630	18,690	19,130	17,880	15,490
Assistant	13,420	13,700	12,640	11,700	15,360	15,670	14,580	13,350
Instructor	11,050	11,260	10,640	10,000	12,550	12,830	11,910	11,190
All ranks[a]	14,560	14,940	13,550	12,080	16,560	16,970	15,630	13,740
Category IIB								
Professor	16,730	17,200	18,680	15,450	19,110	19,070	21,840	17,610
Associate	13,420	14,690	14,200	12,640	15,340	16,610	16,450	14,430
Assistant	11,550	12,360	11,930	10,940	13,160	13,980	13,760	12,450
Instructor	9,900	10,350	10,280	9,460	11,140	11,710	11,690	10,540
All ranks[a]	12,070	12,570	12,890	11,450	13,750	14,170	14,910	13,010

Table 4-6 (continued)

Weighted Average Salaries and Average Compensations for Women Faculty Members, by Category, Type of Affiliation, and Academic Rank, 1974-75

Academic Rank	Salary				Compensation			
	All Combined	Public	Private Independent	Church Related	All Combined	Public	Private Independent	Church Related
Category III								
Professor	$19,790	$20,060	$ —	$ —	$22,490	$22,800	$ —	$ —
Associate	16,290	16,600	11,520	11,280	18,620	18,970	13,290	12,800
Assistant	13,920	14,050	10,580	9,860	16,030	16,190	12,070	11,010
Instructor	11,200	11,440	7,700	8,880	12,770	13,070	8,600	9,740
All ranks[a]	13,720	13,950	9,460	9,640	15,710	15,980	10,730	10,730
Category IV								
No rank	13,630	13,770	12,490	9,310	15,240	15,390	14,260	10,440

[a]Because of the weight any given rank may have, the "All ranks" (overall) average figure should be used with caution.

Note: Sample includes 1,351 institutions providing data by sex. Thus, the base is different from that of Table 4-5. Dashes indicate that sample was too small to be meaningful.

Source: Reprinted with permission from the *AAUP Bulletin*, 61 (Summer 1975), Table 22, p. 138.

Table 4-7
Weighted Average Salaries and Average Compensations for Men Faculty Members, by Category, Type of Affiliation, and Academic Rank, 1974–75

Academic Rank	Salary				Compensation			
	All Combined	Public	Private Independent	Church Related	All Combined	Public	Private Independent	Church Related
Category I								
Professor	$22,990	$22,750	$24,680	$20,900	$26,060	$25,590	$28,870	$23,680
Associate	16,900	16,980	17,260	16,220	19,150	19,070	19,960	18,510
Assistant	13,950	14,000	13,870	13,390	15,860	15,890	15,920	15,270
Instructor	11,070	11,080	10,970	11,120	12,580	12,620	12,270	12,620
All ranks[a]	18,090	17,970	19,310	16,630	20,520	20,280	22,420	18,910
Category IIA								
Professor	21,290	21,680	20,540	18,290	24,110	24,430	23,940	21,050
Associate	16,690	16,950	16,110	14,930	19,050	19,300	18,690	17,160
Assistant	13,850	14,060	13,310	12,600	15,830	16,060	15,310	14,440
Instructor	11,550	11,730	11,210	10,450	13,160	13,400	12,640	11,780
All ranks[a]	16,730	17,040	15,970	14,670	19,040	19,350	18,480	16,840
Category IIB								
Professor	17,860	18,290	19,360	16,890	20,570	20,410	22,470	19,610
Associate	14,320	15,390	14,770	13,560	16,460	17,400	17,090	15,670
Assistant	12,160	12,970	12,430	11,590	13,890	14,730	14,270	13,260
Instructor	10,410	10,790	10,840	9,950	11,740	12,210	12,280	11,160
All ranks[a]	14,000	14,400	14,860	13,360	16,050	16,270	17,150	15,380

Table 4-7 (continued)
Weighted Average Salaries and Average Compensations for Men Faculty Members, by Category, Type of Affiliation, and Academic Rank, 1974-75

Academic Rank	Salary				Compensation			
	All Combined	Public	Private Independent	Church Related	All Combined	Public	Private Independent	Church Related
				Category III				
Professor	$20,430	$20,540	$ —	$ —	$23,300	$23,430	$ —	$ —
Associate	16,480	16,610	12,370	12,000	18,840	18,990	14,350	13,650
Assistant	14,020	14,120	11,010	9,970	16,140	16,260	12,810	11,200
Instructor	11,740	11,900	7,760	8,950	13,360	13,550	8,700	9,860
All ranks[a]	15,000	15,140	10,230	10,360	17,170	17,340	11,750	11,650
				Category IV				
No Rank	14,980	15,100	13,260	9,670	16,760	16,870	15,440	10,930

[a]Because of the weight any given rank may have, the "All ranks" (overall) average figure should be used with caution.

Note: Sample includes 1,351 institutions providing data by sex. Thus, the base is different from that of Table 4-5. Dashes indicate that sample was too small to be meaningful.

Source: Reprinted with permission from the *AAUP Bulletin*, 61 (Summer 1975), Table 23, p. 138.

evaluations. In sum, the salary differentials which appear in Tables 4-5 through 4-7 are a cause for concern; nonetheless, they are not firm evidence of sex discrimination against female faculty.

The most creditable study of sex discrimination in academic salaries that pertains to academia in general has been performed by Bayer and Astin.[13] The Bayer-Astin study is superior to the usual salary surveys (such as the AAUP salary survey) because it is based upon micro-level observations of individual faculty and also because explicit allowance is made for differing productivities of individual faculty. By way of contrast, the annual AAUP salary survey is based upon data which are aggregated at the institutional level and which contain no measures of faculty productivity and performance other than academic rank.

Bayer and Astin point out that male and female academics differ in terms of the variables that have traditionally been the criteria for advancement in higher education. For example, using the American Council on Education general-purpose study of over 53,000 faculty in the 1972-73 academic year, Bayer and Astin found that almost twice as many male academics possessed the Ph.D. degree as did female academics.[14] Similarly, almost twice as many male academics reported having published a book as did female academics.[15] Bayer and Astin also contended that the proportion of women faculty at an institution depends at least partially upon the characteristics of that institution, for example, its requirements for the production of scholarly productivity. In this latter regard, Astin earlier found that women job candidates tended to make voluntary labor market choices which would place them in colleges and universities with lower requirements in the area of scholarly productivity.[16]

The empirical work of Bayer and Astin emphasized a comparison of the results of the aforementioned 1972-73 academic year survey with a similar survey conducted of the 1968-69 academic year. Of the 53,000+ faculty members who participated in the 1972-73 study, Bayer and Astin selected a random sample of approximately 5,000 faculty members to examine in detail. Their basic salary-estimating equation was specified as follows:

$$\$_i = f(D_{ij}, E_{ik}, P_{il}, C_{im})$$ (4.1)

where $i = 1, 2, \ldots, 5{,}000$
$j = 1, 2, \ldots, 10$
$k = 1, 2, \ldots, 7$
$l = 1, 2, \ldots, 11$
$m = 1, 2, \ldots, 5$

and where

$\$$ = salary of faculty member rounded to nearest thousand

D = Ten different demographic characteristics of the faculty member: sex, age, race, father's education, mother's education, citizenship, religious commitment, political orientation, marital status, and parenthood

E = Seven different educational characteristics of the faculty member: highest degree held, field of specialization of highest degree, length of time since receipt of highest degree, receipt of financial aid in graduate school, rating of degree-granting graduate school on a scale of 1 to 9

P = Eleven different professional characteristics of the faculty member: teaching department, years of continuous service at present institution, amount of time spent in administration, teaching, research, interruption of career, number of published articles, number of published books, outside consulting activities, salary year basis

C = Five different characteristics of the faculty member's employing institution: type, control, racial composition, sex composition, geographic location

Based upon the results of their stepwise multiple linear regressions, Bayer and Astin concluded that there was less evidence of sex discrimination against female faculty in the 1972-73 academic year than in the 1968-69 academic year. For example, the two researchers found the partial correlation coefficient between femaleness and academic rank to have fallen from –0.17 to –0.13 in the three-year period between the two surveys.[17] Held constant in this analysis were all the other explanatory variables found in Equation (4.1), such as scholarly productivity. The partial correlation coefficient between femaleness and tenure was 0.014 and not statistically significant at the 0.01 level in the 1972-73 survey year.[18]

Bayer and Astin found the mean salary of male academics to be over $3,000 greater than the mean salary of female academics.[19] However, they could explain only 22 percent of the variance of salaries between and among individual faculty by means of their model.

On the basis of their findings concerning the partial relationship between academic salaries and sex, Bayer and Astin argue that academic rank should not ordinarily be included as an explanatory variable in a sex discrimination study in academia because academic rank is tainted by discriminatory practices. For example, Bayer and Astin demonstrate that the partial correlation coefficient between femaleness and salary is –0.043 when academic rank is included as a control variable, but rises to –0.05 when academic rank is excluded from the analysis.[20] These results, suggest Bayer and Astin, indicate that ". . . the sex differential in salary is due in part to differences in rates of promotion to rank."[21]

Bayer and Astin also found that the relationship between sex and salaries was much weaker at the entry-level positions in academia, such as instructor and assistant professor. This is consistent with the recent findings of Cartter and Ruhter concerning the apparent disappearance of sex discrimination in employment against females in entry-level academic positions in the past few years.[22]

The work of Bayer and Astin also includes a factual-counterfactual analysis in which they estimate what female faculty would have earned had they been paid according to the determinants of male faculty salaries. To this end, they estimated Equation (4.1) for the men in their sample, and then used the estimated regression coefficients to generate a counterfactual estimate of what women would have earned had they been treated the same as men. Bayer and Astin found a $600 deficit between the mean actual salary of female faculty and their mean counterfactual salary when academic rank was included in the analysis.[23] The deficit rose to $1,040 when the influence of academic rank was excluded.[24] The two researchers found virtually no difference between the mean academic ranks of female faculty and the mean counterfactual estimate of their rank. Bayer and Astin concluded that ". . . equity in salary between men and women has been virtually achieved in the junior ranks while differentials persist in the senior ranks."[25]

Despite some inevitable deficiencies, the Bayer-Astin study is easily the most valid and reliable evidence that we have concerning sex discrimination in faculty salaries on a nationwide level. Bayer and Astin do take into consideration a large number of individual faculty characteristics such as scholarly productivity, experience, time spent on the job, and so forth. Such factors are all too often omitted when sex discrimination studies are performed, even when the sample is limited to a particular university or academic department.

An important deficiency of the Bayer-Astin study is the omission of any direct measure of teaching competence and performance from their analysis. This is unfortunate, particularly in view of the strong tendency of a large majority of academic institutions to stress this feature of faculty performance far more than scholarly productivity. The blunt fact is that there is relatively little published scholarly productivity of repute being generated in most of the 3,000+ institutions of higher education in the United States. Hence, it is not accurate to suggest, in the fashion of Bayer and Astin, that performance in scholarly productivity is the traditional basis for salary decisions and promotions. The omission leads to a possible misspecification. It also may introduce in the analysis a subtle bias against female faculty. If, as Astin contends, female faculty often willingly choose an institution where their major duties are teaching rather than the generation of publications, then it follows that an analysis which ignores teaching and stresses scholarly publications as salary determinants will produce a low estimate of any discrimination that might be present.

The fact that no direct measure of teaching performance and competence appears in the equation estimated by Bayer and Astin is regrettable, though quite understandable. It is hardly possible to collect reliable information on the teaching of 53,000+ faculty members by means of a survey. This is an argument in favor of limiting sex discrimination studies to a particular academic institution where there is greater likelihood of obtaining valid estimates of the teaching competence of individual faculty. The same criticism may hold true, although to a lesser extent, with respect to the evaluation of the service and committee work of individual faculty, which Bayer and Astin also do not consider.

The propensity of Bayer and Astin to utilize arbitrary qualitative variables instead of multiple-category dummy variables is also subject to criticism. For example, with respect to academic rank, Bayer and Astin assign a value of 1 to instructor status, 2 to assistant-professor status, 3 to associate-professor status, and 4 to full-processor status. In so doing, they impose a structure upon the relationship of academic rank to performance that may not actually exist. It does not follow that a full professor is 4 times as productive, or 4 times as anything, as an instructor. Each academic rank should be represented by its own dummy variable, so that no arbitrary structure is imposed upon the data. Hence, if a particular faculty member is an associate professor, a value of 1 would be assigned to the associate-professor variable, while values of 0 would be assigned to the instructor, assistant-professor, and full-professor variables in this particular case. Four different dummy variables should exist for academic rank, not just one.

Finally, Bayer and Astin do not take into account possible sex differences in labor force participation rates, quit rates, and expected future productivities. If such differences do exist, then sex salary differentials may develop at the entry-level academic ranks as well as the upper-level ranks without this being evidence of sex discrimination. Seemingly identically qualified individuals might well receive differing entry-level salaries. This, however, is a complicated matter worthy of considerable additional discussion, which we will undertake in the next two sections.

Sex Discrimination Studies: Specific Universities

Studies of faculty salary determination at particular universities have become commonplace in recent years. Among the earliest of those which contain reliable controls for differential faculty productivity and performance is that performed by Siegfried and White concerning the department of economics at the University of Wisconsin, Madison.[26] Siegfried and White attempted to explain interfaculty variations in individual salaries on the basis of faculty experience, publications, teaching competence, and administrative duties. That is,

$$\$_i = f(Y_i, P_i, T_i, A_i) \qquad (i = 1, 2, \ldots, 45) \qquad (4.2)$$

where $\$$ = academic-year salary in dollars
Y = years of experience
P = publications in four categories: monographs, national journal articles, specialty journal articles, other
T = teaching rate assigned by students
A = administrative duties

Siegfried and White utilized multiple linear regression and found that publications and administrative duties had the greatest influence on the salaries of the Madison economists. There was no attempt to deal with the possibility of sex discrimination in salaries.

The first reliable published study of faculty salaries at a particular university that dealt with the issue of sex discrimination was that performed by Katz at the University of Illinois.[27] Katz examined the salaries of 596 full-time professors in eleven different academic departments in the 1969-70 academic year. Multiple linear regression was once again the tool, as Katz estimated the following equation:

$$\$_i = f(NB_i, NA_i, NEA_i, T_i, DS_i, S_i, C_i, D_i, U_i, G_i, A_i, F_i, P_i)$$

$$(i = 1, 2, \ldots, 596) \qquad (4.3)$$

where $\$$ = yearly salary in dollars
NB = number of books published
NA = number of articles published
NEA = number of excellent articles published
T = dummy variable representing superior teaching ability
DS = dissertations supervised
S = dummy variable representing public service
C = dummy variable representing committee work
D = dummy variable representing academic department of particular faculty member
U = dummy variable representing quality of undergraduate school where faculty member obtained degree
G = dummy variable representing quality of graduate school where faculty member obtained degree
A = dummy variable representing administrative appointment
F = dummy variable representing sex of faculty member
P = dummy variable representing whether faculty member has Ph.D. degree

Katz found that the major payoffs to faculty in terms of salary were books published, the number of excellent journal articles, dissertation supervision, and an administrative appointment. A tax of $2,410 existed (*ceteris paribus*) on femaleness. Katz then constructed a cardinal index of scholarly productivity which had a mean value of 846 for men faculty and a mean value of 261 for female faculty.[28] He concluded that ". . . even after taking into consideration their lower productivity, women are still paid less than men."[29]

The Katz study is notable for its consideration of the differential productivity of faculty. The only apparent deficiency in this area is the variable representing teaching competence which was based primarily upon the oral tradition and rumor rather than on the results of a consistent and controlled application of a teacher-evaluation instrument.

The major deficiency of the Katz study is one which is common to nearly all cross-sectional studies. Possible differentials in labor force participation rates, absences of work, quit rates, specific human capital, and peer evaluations between the sexes are ignored. Such factors could account for salary differentials between faculty members with identical scholarly productivity. If, for example, quit rates are higher for female faculty, then the cost of maintaining a teaching staff and hiring replacements is greater when the proportion of female faculty is greater. This would tend to lower the expected net lifetime productivity of female faculty and therefore their wages.

The "specificity" of female human capital would also tend to be lessened by factors such as lower labor force participation rates and higher quit rates. "Specific" human capital is knowledge specific to a particular university—"knowing the ropes."[30] Presumably those faculty with greater experience and uninterrupted careers at a particular university have more specific human capital. Hence, they will, *ceteris paribus*, receive a higher wage. As Landes has argued, less specific human capital is ". . . a sufficient reason for wage differentials to exist, even in the absence of any taste for discrimination by employers, co-workers, or customers."[31]

The problem of the evaluation of teaching competence, and its effects upon faculty salaries, was dealt with directly by Koch and Chizmar.[32] Koch and Chizmar attempted to explain interfaculty variations in salaries for 229 faculty members in sixteen arts and sciences departments at Illinois State University for the year 1972-73. For the first time also, the determinants of salary increments were inspected as well. The measure of teaching competence was assigned by an elected committee of peers in each faculty member's department as a part of a regularly scheduled annual evaluation process. The peer evaluations relied heavily upon student evaluations of teaching carried out by the committee of peers.

Koch and Chizmar utilized a multiple linear regression equation specified as follows:

$$\$_i = f(T_i, SP_i, S_i, R_i, M_i, Y_i, P_i, SX_i, R_i) \qquad (i = 1, 2, \ldots, 229) \quad (4.4)$$

and

$$\Delta\$_i = f(T_i, SP_i, S_i, R_i, M_i, X_i, P_i, SX_i, R_i) \qquad (i = 1, 2, \ldots, 229) \quad (4.5)$$

where $\$$ = monthly salary in dollars
$\Delta\$$ = monthly salary increment in dollars
T = multiple-category dummy variable reflecting evaluated teaching competence
SP = multiple-category dummy variable reflecting evaluated competence in scholarly productivity
S = multiple-category dummy variable reflecting evaluated competence in service
R = multiple-category dummy variable reflecting academic rank
M = multiple-category dummy variable reflecting market situation in a particular discipline
Y = years faculty member was in possession of Ph.D. degree
SX = dummy variable reflecting sex of faculty member
R = dummy variable reflecting race of faculty member

Koch and Chizmar found that academic rank and years of experience were statistically significant predictors of absolute faculty salaries at Illinois State University. Merit evaluations of each faculty member's productivity by peers were not statistically significant predictors. The partial regression coefficient on the sex variable revealed a $69 penalty per month upon femaleness. This coefficient was statistically significant at the 0.01 level in a two-tailed test.

By way of contrast, the peer evaluations of each faculty member's productivity were highly significant predictors of salary increments. Sex was not a statistically significant predictor of salary increments. Koch and Chizmar concluded that a visible change in salary policy had occurred at Illinois State University over time such that faculty were now being rewarded more upon the basis of evaluated performance than on longevity.

The Koch-Chizmar study is liable to the same criticisms as the Katz study with respect to not considering the effects of differences in labor force participation rates, quit rates, expected future productivity, and sexist peer evaluations. It is notable primarily because it features peer evaluations of faculty productivity and, in particular, because it incorporates a standardized evaluation of each faculty member's teaching competence. This latter point is particularly important in the mass of institutions of higher education which do not stress and/or require scholarly publication by their faculty. A simple count of articles and books in a typical non-publish-or-perish academic institution is a faulty measure of faculty performance.

The University of Illinois was once again the site of a sex discrimination study, this one reported by Ferber.[33] Returned questionnaires from faculty, 278 in number (about 75 percent of those originally approached for information), were the basis of a study of the faculty salary structure at the University of Illinois in the academic year 1969-70. Multiple linear regression of the following form was used:

$$\$_i = f(D_i, R_i, Y_i, DE_i, PUB_i, EXP_i, H_i, CS_i, MS_i, CH_i, SE_i)$$

$$(i = 1, 2, \ldots, 278) \qquad\qquad\qquad (4.6)$$

where D = faculty member's academic department
         R = faculty member's academic rank
         Y = years in rank
        DE = degree status
       PUB = publications
       EXP = years experience
         H = honors received
        CS = dummy variable representing contract status (9 or 11 months)
        MS = dummy variable representing marital status
        CH = number of children
        SE = dummy variable indicating whether spouse is employed by the university

Ferber found that faculty who were married to another faculty member tended to be treated as one income-earning unit. For example, if a woman's husband was also employed by the university, that woman's salary was significantly lower as a result. Scholarly productivity was not found to be important, although the Ferber measure of scholarly productivity was hardly exact. In general, the Ferber study is in most ways inferior to the Katz study at the same institution and does not add much to our knowledge except for the finding with respect to income-earning wife-husband teams. This may be indirect evidence concerning sex differences, labor force participation rates, quit rates, and expected future productivity. It is clearly consistent with the wage-discriminating monopsonist model.

An important and differentiated approach to the issue of sex discrimination was carried out at Southern Methodist University by Reagan and Maynard.[34] The major innovations of Reagan and Maynard were twofold. First, they totally ignored the influence of academic rank upon salaries, arguing that rank at Southern Methodist University has been contaminated by sex discrimination against female faculty. Second, they grouped academic fields together that have similar entrance salaries for beginning assistant professors with Ph.D. degrees.

They then followed the progress of individual faculty members in these departments with respect to salary growth, promotion, and tenure.

Reagan and Maynard found that about 75 percent of women faculty at Southern Methodist University had salaries below men with corresponding credentials in terms of their internal labor market analysis.[35] The salary differential ranged from 5 to 50 percent at various levels.[36] Ultimately, 54 of the 64 women faculty studied received a total of $1,135 per month on a 9-month basis because of sex discrimination.[37]

The Reagan-Maynard study assumed that the assistant-professor rank is the major "entry port" for a typical professor. At such a level, the salaries of male and female professors should be the same once the influence of the outside market has been taken into account. In comparing male and female faculty, Reagan and Maynard took into account the degree status of the faculty member, the prestige of the faculty member's degree-granting graduate school, years in academic rank, an eight-class index of scholarly productivity, and the percent of the faculty member's salary recovered from externally funded grants and contracts. No measure of teaching competence was utilized, nor was any consideration given to possible differentials between male and female faculty in terms of labor force participation rates, quit rates, generalized expected lifetime productivity, or peer evaluations. However, even should such factors be taken into account, Reagan and Maynard argue that the observed salary differentials between men and women faculty at Southern Methodist University reflected sex discrimination.

Sex Discrimination Studies: Specific Academic Disciplines

One of the most careful and most interesting studies of sex discrimination in specific academic disciplines has been conducted by Johnson and Stafford.[38] Johnson and Stafford suggest that male and female life-cycle income patterns may be different because of voluntary labor market choices made by males and females. Johnson and Stafford, following Ben-Porath,[39] Rosen,[40] and others, see the wages of female faculty members declining relative to those of males during child-bearing years; however, in subsequent years this differential should narrow. Lower labor force participation and higher quit rates are important reasons for the appearance of the differential.[41]

Johnson and Stafford also placed some reliance upon the "specific" human-capital hypothesis noted earlier. If the human capital of female faculty members is less specific because of labor force participation and quit rates, then they will, *ceteris paribus*, earn less than male faculty with similar other qualifications.

The argument was also developed by Johnson and Stafford (and borrowed from Ben-Porath) that female academics will tend to choose (disproportionately) less prestigious academic institutions where initial salaries are high, but levels of scholarship and intellectual activity are lower. Johnson and Stafford argued that this applies to female academics who voluntarily forego the higher rate of skill improvement that would occur at a prestigious institution and instead opt for a higher present-year salary.[42] Hence, female academics should have flatter lifetime-earnings profiles because they give up on the job training in exchange for a higher present-year wage.

The life-cycle income hypothesis of Johnson and Stafford was subjected to testing by means of data derived from the National Science Foundation Register of Scientific and Technical Personnel for the year 1970. Ph.D. holders in six academic disciplines (anthropology, biology, economics, mathematics, physics, and sociology) were in the data set. Johnson and Stafford concentrated upon experience, the quality of the individual's graduate degree-granting school, citizenship, and sex to explain earnings differentials observed in a given discipline. The functional form of their linear regression format is worthy of discussion.

$$\ln \$_i = f(XPO_i, XPO_i^2, XPR_i, XPR_i^2, XPO_i \cdot XPR_i, NC_i, RNKD_i,$$

$$FEM_i, FEM_i \cdot XPO, FEM_i \cdot XPO_i^2, FEM_i \cdot RNKD_i,$$

$$FEM_i \cdot XPR_i, FEM_i \cdot XPR_i^2) \quad (i = 1, 2, \ldots, N) \qquad (4.7)$$

where XPO = postdegree experience in years
        XPR = predegree experience in years
        NC = dummy variable indicating faculty member is not a citizen of the United States
        $RNKD$ = dummy variable indicating quality of faculty member's degree-granting graduate school
        FEM = dummy variable indicating faculty member is female

The interaction terms of the Johnson-Stafford regression model are a direct implication of the life-cycle earnings hypothesis. Interactions are expected between variables representing sex and those representing experience that would not be caught by the individual regression coefficients of the sex and experience variables. Hence, a variable such as $FEM \cdot XPO$ is designed to pick up this interaction. Note also, however, that allowance is made for possible nonlinear relationships between salary and predegree experience (XPR) and postdegree experience (XPO). The XPR^2 and XPO^2 terms recognize this possibility.[a]

Holding constant other variables, Johnson and Stafford find that the

---

[a]Johnson and Stafford feel that extensive predegree experience will result in a flatter life-cycle earnings profile because an individual with extensive predegree experience will already have a fairly high salary when she or he gets the degree.

differential between male and female salaries grows most during the time period characterized by 5 to 15 years of postdegree experience and narrows thereafter. For example, with 0 years of postdegree experience, the ratio of female salaries to male salaries in economics is 0.947 (*ceteris paribus*). This ratio falls to 0.857 with 15 years of postdegree experience, and rebounds slightly thereafter.[43]

Johnson and Stafford found that the interaction terms they specified in their model added little explanatory power. Similarly, the quality of the graduate school from which the faculty member had, graduated seemed to have little relationship to earnings.

The flatter earnings profile for women discovered by Johnson and Stafford is consistent with their life-cycle hypothesis. It is also consistent with the assertion that female academics will tend to choose those places of employment where extensive scholarly research is not required. This is supportive of the earlier cited findings of Helen Astin concerning women doctorate holders in general.[44]

While the life-cycle earnings hypothesis suggests that much of the observed earnings differentials between female and male faculty members is due to differences in training and especially due to voluntary labor market choices, the Johnson-Stafford empirical results also point to a residual of sex discrimination in salaries. Male academics have salaries which, at 0 years of postdegree experience, average 6.9 percent higher than comparable female academics. This gap more than doubles at 15 years postdegree experience.[45] The 6.9 percent differential may be a measure of discrimination according to Johnson and Stafford. They conclude, however, that well over one-half of the observed differential in salaries observed between male and female academics with the same outward credentials is due to voluntary labor market choices by those men and women.[46]

The Johnson-Stafford study is carefully done; yet it does not permit us to determine precisely why the life-cycle earnings profiles of male and female Ph.D. holders differ. The differential may be due to discrimination; but, on the other hand, it may not be. For example, the 6.9 percent salary differential noted at 0 years of postdegree experience could possibly be the result of sex differentials in expected lifetime productivity rather than discrimination. If an employer expects a female faculty member to drop out of the labor force, have a higher quit rate, be absent more often, and so forth, then this is a sufficient reason to expect lower lifetime productivity on the part of that female. It also implies that the university may have to bear costs in order to recruit a replacement. New faculty members especially are recruited on the basis of their expected future performance and productivity. If, in general, the expected future productivity of female faculty members is less than that for male faculty with comparable credentials, then there is an economic (though probably illegal) rationale for a lower wage to be paid to the typical female faculty member. Such a behavior may not coincide with the normative preferences of a large number of individuals. Economists have no special competence in the arena of normative conclusions, however.

Conclusions concerning the propriety of such employer behavior must therefore be left to the dictates of the reader's conscience.

One infers from the findings of Johnson and Stafford that female academics have lower labor force participation rates, and higher quit rates, than comparable male academics. It is important to observe, however, that the Johnson-Stafford data set does not include any direct information on the labor force participation or quit rates of specific male or female faculty. Johnson and Stafford quote evidence in these areas that is generally supportive of the life-cycle earnings hypothesis. None of this evidence, however, relates directly to the faculty members included in their data set. It is impossible to connect the salary of a particular faculty member to a particular labor force participation pattern.

An additional criticism of some import of the Johnson-Stafford study is that the regression equations do not include, except indirectly, any measures of individual faculty performance and productivity. Johnson and Stafford attempt to approximate productivity and performance by years of experience and the quality of the graduate school where the faculty member obtained his or her degree. Neither of these measures particularly commends itself as a measure of productivity. In any case, Johnson and Stafford found no relation between the prestige of the degree-granting school and faculty salaries. Once again, from the Johnson and Stafford results one might well infer lower productivity and performance by the representative female faculty member. Nonetheless, such a conclusion does not logically follow from their findings and cannot be supported except in the most general sense by their data set.

Studies of Affirmative Action Salary Programs

Affirmative action salary programs have become commonplace both inside and outside academia. Nevertheless, we know relatively little about the actual operation and effects of these programs, because those in charge of such programs have placed strong emphasis upon not divulging individual affirmative action salary payments. In general, when the existence of an affirmative action salary program is acknowledged, only broadly aggregative data are given to those who wish to examine the operation and effects of that program. "X dollars were given to Y individuals" is the typical report. This, however, makes it virtually impossible to reach any conclusions about the efficacy and effects of the affirmative action program.

In only two cases have sufficient data been made available such that an affirmative action program could be analyzed in detail. In one case, that involving the University of Nebraska, the data have come to light only because of a legal suit and judicial decision. The data would not have been disclosed voluntarily. The other case involves the authors of this book and Illinois State

University. It suffices to note that administrators have typically chosen the path of least resistance and have opted in favor of secrecy. External monitoring of affirmative action salary programs is infrequent, and when it has occurred, it has seldom been meaningful.

A potentially far-reaching judicial decision has been reached in the case of *Regents* v. *Dawes* (1975).[47] In the spring of 1972, the University of Nebraska became concerned over its own possible violation of Title VII of the Civil Rights Act of 1964. The university determined to eliminate any salary discrimination that might have existed against female faculty there. As a result, the colleges of agriculture and home economics appointed a joint committee to consider the matter and to recommend possible action.

The appointed committee decided that it would be impossible to match comparable men and women in all cases. Therefore, the decision was made to develop a formula which would generate a "predicted salary" for each female faculty member. The predicted salary was counterfactual in nature and reflected the faculty member's years of experience, education, specialization, and merit. This predicted salary was then compared to the female faculty member's actual salary in order to obtain an estimate of sex discrimination.

For "specialist" staff on the university campus, the predicted salary for a given female faculty member was produced by the following formula:

$$\text{Predicted salary} = A + B + \frac{[(3 \times C) + (1.5 \times D)] \times \$106}{E} \qquad (4.8)$$

where A = value of educational level in terms of dollars
        B = value of years of specialization in terms of dollars
        C = years of direct experience
        D = years of related experience
        E = merit rating of faculty member on a scale of 1 through 5, with
              1 being the best and 5 the worst

The value of doctoral degree to a faculty member with no years of experience was taken to be $14,000 annually. It can be observed in Equation (4.8) that each year of direct experience was worth ($106 × 3)/1 = $318 annually to someone who had received the most favorable ("1") merit rating. On the other hand, each year of direct experience was worth only ($106 × 3)/5 = $63.60 per year to someone who had received the lowest ("5") merit rating. Years of related job experience were given precisely one-half the weight of the equivalent number of years of direct experience.

On the basis of the arbitrary weights assigned to the variables represented in Equation (4.8), a predicted salary was generated for each of 272 male faculty members and each of 125 female faculty members. Of the 272 males 92

(34 percent) were found to have had actual salaries below the counterfactual predicted salary, while 33 of the 125 females (26 percent) were found to have had salaries less than their counterfactual predicted salary. Effective July 1, 1972, the salaries of the 33 female faculty members were raised to the counter-factual formula level; however, no action was taken with respect to the salaries of the 92 male faculty who were also found to have had salaries below the counterfactual formula level.

A legal suit was brought against the Board of Regents of the University of Nebraska on behalf of the 92 male faculty members whose salaries were found to be below the counterfactual formula level. The U.S. District Court, State of Nebraska, heard the case and decided it in favor of the Board of Regents. The university was not required to provide any additional salary monies for the 92 male faculty. On appeal, however, this judgment was reversed by the Eighth Circuit Court of Appeals, primarily on the ground that the affirmative action salary procedure had violated the Equal Pay Act of 1963.

The Equal Pay Act of 1963 prohibits the use of salary schedules or any other compensation technique which is not applied in an even-handed fashion to all individuals. The Equal Pay Act does not require that all employees receive equal pay—only that the same criteria and pay standards be applied to all employees. The Appeals court found that the sole factor responsible for increasing the salaries of the 33 female faculty rather than the salaries of the 92 male faculty was sex and that the procedure therefore was not permissible. The court did not hold that the University of Nebraska must operate an affirma-tive action program, nor did it rule in favor of salary schedules of minimum-salary levels. Rather, the decision of the Appeals court established only that it is unlawful to operate an affirmative action salary program where the eligibility for benefits is limited to one sex or race.

The implications of *Regents* v. *Dawes* for affirmative action programs are immense. Affirmative action programs and affirmative action officers have seldom exhibited long-term interest in the existence of possible discrimination against male and/or nonminority faculty. Hence, most affirmative action pro-grams have at least potentially violated the Equal Pay Act of 1963 at the same time that they have used the Equal Pay Act as a basis for the elimination of sex or race discrimination. *Regents* v. *Dawes* states clearly that affirmative action based upon the Equal Pay Act must apply to all faculty, regardless of sex or race.

An irony of the *Regents* v. *Dawes* decision is that the salary formula utilized by the University of Nebraska was defective from many standpoints, even though it satisfied the dictates of the law. The formula described in Equation (4.8) arbitrarily specified weights upon factors such as degree status and years of experience. The validity of these weights in terms of how University of Nebraska faculty were actually being paid is unknown. Affirma-tive action salary programs should be based upon how faculty are actually paid rather than someone's best guess about how they believe it to be. The arbitrary weights chosen by the University of Nebraska committee may have been biased for or against female faculty relative to the way faculty are actually paid at the university. It is impossible to determine which is the case. The use of a hypothetical, though well-meaning, counterfactual salary criterion may be better than having no counterfactual salary criterion at all. However, a counterfactual salary based upon coefficients produced by a valid estimation procedure is clearly preferable.

It is clear nonetheless that the defectiveness of the committee formula was never really at issue in *Regents* v. *Dawes*. However capricious the formula might have been, the procedure as such would have gone unchallenged by the Appeals court had the salary implications of the formula been applied to both male and female faculty. The lesson is that the same formula must be applied to all faculty. A university may adopt nearly any standard whatsoever in terms of salary dispensation. That standard, however, must be applied uniformly to all faculty.

The most detailed empirical study of an affirmative action salary program has been carried out by Koch and Chizmar.[48] A factual-counterfactual model (in the fashion of Bayer and Astin) was utilized to generate an estimate of what each female faculty member would have been paid had she been paid according to the determinants of male faculty salaries. This counterfactual estimate for each female faculty member was then compared to the actual salary of the female faculty member in order to obtain an estimate of sex discrimination in salaries. At Illinois State University 530 full-time, nonadministrative faculty (118 females) were the sample upon which the empirical work was based.

The multiple regression format and the variable specification utilized by Koch and Chizmar duplicate that of their earlier cited study as summarized by Equations (4.4) and (4.5). Koch and Chizmar found the mean counterfactual salary of female faculty to be $1,620 per month in the 1973-74 academic year. The actual salary of the same female faculty, however, was only $1,596 per month. The difference between these two salary magnitudes is $24 per month, and might be interpreted as an estimate of mean salary discrimination against female faculty. The difference is not statistically significant at the 0.10 level, however.

The affirmative action salary program undertaken at Illinois State University in 1973-74 increased the mean salary of female faculty to $1,643 per month. The $23 per month post-affirmative-action difference (1,643 - 1,620 = 23) might be interpreted as reverse discrimination against male faculty. This difference, however, also failed to attain statistical significance at the 0.10 level.

Koch and Chizmar spoke of the possibility of faculty and administrators "leaning over backward" in order to avoid any possibility of salary sex discrimination against female faculty. "Leaning over backward" is one possible manner in which to explain the post-affirmative-action difference of $23 per month. We will examine this argument in greater detail in Chapter 5 where the formal empirical analysis of this book is carried out.

The Koch-Chizmar study is detailed in terms of the number of independent variables specified, and it includes three different peer evaluations of each faculty member's productivity. Such peer evaluations, particularly in the area of teaching competence, do not exist in most other studies. On the other hand, both the University of Nebraska case and the Illinois State University case (Koch-Chizmar) lack controls relating to possible sex differences in labor force participation rates, quit rates, expected future productivity, and peer perceptions. These issues have been deferred too long, and will be considered in the next section.

Unresolved Issues

In our review of the existing literature and empirical evidence in the area of sex discrimination and affirmative action, we have repeatedly pointed out that what appears to be the presence (absence) of sex discrimination could be greatly affected by the existence of sex differences in four job-related factors: (1) labor force participation rates, (2) quit rates, (3) expected future productivity, and (4) peer perceptions of performance. We will now consider each of these matters in turn.

Labor Force Participation Rates

To the extent that the labor force participation rates of female academics are lower than those of male academics, it follows that their expected future productivity will (*ceteris paribus*) be lower than that of male academics. Further, the cost of recruiting replacements for female academics will be higher, and therefore employers might well be reluctant to hire female academics. In a different context, absence from the labor force could also be a partial explanation for some of the earnings differentials observed between male and female holders of a certain degree.

The evidence concerning sex differences in labor force participation rates is spotty. Tsuchigane and Dodge report that 1970 Census data reveal that female employees worked fewer hours than male employees.[49] Similarly, Johnson and Stafford have inferred from the 1970 Census data a substantial sex difference in hours worked in academia. Female academics worked an average of 1,200 hours per year, while male academics worked an average of 1,760 hours per year.[50] Neither of these scraps of evidence bears directly upon labor force participation rates, however. More to the point with respect to academia are the results reported by Johnson and Stafford with respect to academics in specific

disciplines. For example, Johnson and Stafford found sex differences in the
percent of men and women Ph.D.-holding biologists who were employed part-
time. In the under-30-years age bracket, 6.3 percent of all male Ph.D.-holding
biologists were employed part-time, while only 5.2 percent of their female
counterparts were employed part-time. In the 30-to-34-year age bracket, however, only 1.1 percent of males were employed part-time, while 11.8 percent
of females were employed part-time. In the 35-to-44-year age bracket, the
male and female part-time percents were 0.5 and 7.2, respectively.[51] Hence,
rather obvious sex differences in labor force participation apparently do occur
among academics. It is logical to expect such sex differences to be reflected
in the market earnings of each sex.

A related matter which does not come directly under the heading of labor
force participation, but nevertheless clearly influences the amount of labor
supplied by females, is absenteeism. The conventional knowledge in this area
is that females will exhibit higher rates of absenteeism because of child and
family responsibilities. There is, however, relatively little evidence to support
this allegation. Utilizing Bureau of Labor Statistics data, Tsuchigane and
Dodge report that the mean number of absentee days per year by male employees was 5.2 in 1970, while the corresponding mean was 5.6 for female
employees.[52] This difference is very small indeed and cannot account for more
than a miniscule portion of observed sex differences in earnings.

Quit Rates

If one sex has a higher quit rate than the other, then the sex with the higher
quit rate is likely to suffer at least two adverse consequences. First, it is likely
that employers ordinarily will be relatively reluctant to hire employees from a
class that has exhibited a high quit rate.[b] Second, since a "quit" imposes costs
upon the employer,[53] it is likely that employees who are associated with a class
of individuals exhibiting a high quit rate will receive lower wages.

Available empirical evidence points to higher quit rates for female employees. In the time period 1950-1955, a mean quit rate of 2.4 per 100 employees
per month was reported for female employees, whereas the corresponding datum
was only 1.8 for male employees.[54] Similar data for 1968 reveal a mean quit
rate of 2.6 for women and 2.2 for men.[55] Other available evidence does not
encourage the proposition that quit rates do not vary between sexes.[56] It should
be noted, however, that none of this evidence relates directly to academia.

------

[b]Exceptions to this dictum might well include seasonal work and jobs where the
employer wishes to preserve the ability to lay off or fire workers without difficulty.

Expected Future Productivity

If the labor force participation rates of female academics are lower, and quit rates higher than those of male academics, then it follows that either there will be fewer female academics hired or that female academics will likely receive lower wages than otherwise comparable male academics. The "specific" human-capital argument of Landes is relevant here. It also follows that the same effects will ordinarily result if female academics make voluntary labor market decisions which tend to discourage their scholarly productivity. This argument has been discussed in detail in an earlier section.

At this point, we must concretely address the question, Are female academics less productive than male academics? The answer to this question may depend upon how one defines productivity. If productivity is defined as publication in the most prestigious scholarly journal outlets, then there is strong evidence that female academics are not as productive as men. Table 4-8 indicates the relative productivity of female scholars in a wide range of academic fields, as compiled by Tsuchigane and Dodge.[57] In every discipline, the percent of scholarly articles emanating from females is substantially lower than the percent of females in that discipline. In economics, for example, approximately 6 percent of the individuals in the discipline are female, but only 1.7 percent of the articles published in the top six journals of the discipline in 1970 were generated by females.

The reasons for the apparent lower scholarly productivity of females are diverse, and may include discrimination by graduate schools, employers, and journal editors. The following factors seem relevant. First, fewer female academics than male academics hold the tenured, full-professor positions that traditionally have been the source of scholarly research. Second, graduate schools may not encourage female students in the direction of scholarly productivity. Instead, there may be subtle emphasis upon supplementing a husband's income. Third, the choice of the graduate school itself by females and the admissions policies of graduate schools may funnel female students away from the most prestigious graduate schools, which traditionally have produced the students who generate the most published research. Fourth, following Astin,[58] females may make voluntary labor market choices not to seek jobs at publish-or-perish institutions; similarly, such institutions may not actively seek female candidates for such positions in any case. Fifth, the burden of children and families may affect work hours, labor force participation, and quit rates, with the end result that the published scholarship of females is lower than that of males. Sixth, discrimination may exist against females at the level of the scholarly journals. It may be more difficult for females to obtain journal article acceptances, or for that matter to obtain grant monies and other perquisites.

The source of the lower scholarly productivity of female academics are

Table 4-8

Percentage of Women in Various Specialties Compared with Percentage of Articles in Related Professional Journals Contributed by Women, 1970

Field	Percentage of Women in Speciality (1)[a]	Percentage of Articles by Women (2)[b]	Ratio (2)/(1) (3)	Sample Size (4)
Natural Sciences				
Mathematics	11	1.3	0.11	5,140
Statistics	11	1.0	0.09	1,455
Computer science	10	2.1	0.21	559
Physics	4	0.3	0.07	1,001
Atmospheric sciences	2	0.2	0.10	800
Earth sciences	3	0.5	0.16	1,882
Chemistry	7	4.4	0.63	924
Biological sciences	13	5.2	0.40	758
Engineering	1	0.1	0.10	930
Social Sciences				
Anthropology	19	8.1	0.44	650
Economics	6	1.7	0.28	638
Political science	10	4.4	0.44	1,125
Psychology	24	9.3	0.38	9,485
Sociology	12	5.6	0.47	5,761
Humanities				
English	50	6.5	0.13	9,105
Plays (theater)	50	12.6	0.25	4.179
History	10	1.5	0.15	2,048
Linguistics	23	2.7	0.12	7,693
Education	25	7.6	0.30	1,649
Law	4	0.2	0.50	668

[a]Derived from *National Register of Scientific and Technical Personnel 1970*, Table A-59, and *College Education Workers 1968-80*.

[b]For the selection of professional journals and method of making article counts, see Appendix A.

Sources: National Science Foundation, *National Register of Scientific and Technical Personnel 1970*, Table A-59; Bureau of Labor Statistics, *College Education Workers 1968-80* (Bulletin 1676, 1970); and selected professional journals in each specialty. Reprinted with permission from Robert Tsuchigane and Norton Dodge, *Economic Discrimination against Women in the United States* (Lexington, Mass.: D.C. Heath, Lexington Books, 1974), Table 4-1, p. 32.

complex and are deeply rooted in the institutions and attitudes of the day. Nonetheless, the evidence does point to a lower expected future productivity by females in the area of published scholarship. While this expectation may assume a self-fulfilling nature, it will tend to cause fewer female academics to be hired and lower wage rates to be paid to those that are hired, even at starting levels. The basic causes which encourage these actions may well be discriminatory; however, the actions themselves are not discriminatory in an economic sense, and they represent efficient behavior in a static sense.

Evidence relating to the teaching competence of female faculty vis-a-vis male faculty is difficult to obtain and interpret. There does not exist a consensus concerning what characterizes good teaching or how one might measure such. There are virtually no nationwide data concerning the relative teaching competency of male and female academics. Table 4-9 presents localized data concerning evaluated teaching competence of faculty at Illinois State University. Each year an elected committee of departmental faculty peers at Illinois State University evaluates the teaching competence of each faculty member in terms of one of four ordinal rankings: inadequate, some merit, considerable merit, and unusual merit.[c] Table 4-9 reports the percents of male and female faculty who were assigned these ratings for the academic year 1973-74.

It is not clear from Table 4-9 that any pervasive sex differences exist in the competence of the teaching of professors at Illinois State University. If an "inadequate" rating is assigned a cardinal value of 0,[d] and "some merit," "considerable merit," and "unusual merit" are assigned cardinal values of 1, 2, and 3, respectively, then we find that the mean competency evaluation for male faculty is 2.14 (standard deviation = 0.71), while the mean competency evaluation of the teaching of female faculty is 2.13 (standard deviation = 0.79). Hence, the limited evidence available does not encourage the view that there exist sex differences in teaching competency. This is important since the vast majority of academic institutions of the United States pay little more than lip service to the generation of scholarly productivity. In most academic institutions, advancement seems most often to reflect faithful service, perceived teaching ability, and personality considerations rather than published scholarship.

---

[c]The elected faculty committees seem to place a strong weight upon student evaluations of each professor's teaching in terms of reaching a decision about which merit evaluation to assign to a particular faculty member.

[d]Strictly speaking, this is not a legitimate practice since it arbitrarily imposes on the various merit evaluations a value structure that may not actually exist. For example, there is no reason to feel that "considerable merit" is twice as good as "some merit," nor is there any valid way to interpret what they would mean if it were true.

Table 4-9
Percent of Male and Female Faculty at Illinois State University Receiving Various Peer Evaluations of Teaching Competence, 1973-74

Peer Evaluation of Teaching Competence	Percent of Male Faculty	Percent of Female Faculty
Inadequate	0	1
Some Merit	19	22
Considerable Merit	48	40
Unusual Merit	33	37

Note: A total of 530 full-time, nonadministrative faculty are included in the sample. Of these faculty 118 were female. The peer evaluations ordinarily placed high reliance upon student evaluations of the teaching competence of each individual faculty member.

Peer Perceptions of Performance

At the heart of the sex discrimination argument is the contention by many that females are not evaluated fairly. Given the same performances or journal articles by a male and a female, the male's performance and contribution will frequently receive a superior evaluation by judges and referees of both sexes. Or, a vita or inquiry submitted by a male job candidate is reacted to more favorably than precisely the same vita or inquiry by a female job candidate.[59]

To the extent that basic peer perceptions and evaluations of females are discriminatory in nature, females will appear to be less meritorious and less productive than their male counterparts. Additionally, they will be given fewer resources, fewer journal article acceptances, fewer promotions, and so forth. Hence, most of the studies of sex discrimination will understate the actual amount of sex discrimination present.

It is difficult to do anything about the possibility of biased peer perceptions of females other than to state it as an important and meaningful caveat. Since there is evidence that there are differences in peer perceptions of individuals and their productivity according to sex, we must constantly be aware of the possible effects of this upon our empirical studies. The strength of any conclusions reached may be attenuated by this type of phenomenon.

Summary

Possible sex differences in labor force participation, quit rates, expected future productivity, and peer perceptions of performance exist. These factors are seldom taken into account in all but the most aggregative sex discrimination studies. The inclusion of such factors might well alter the conclusions of many studies. These factors will not be included in the empirical results reported in Chapter 5 except in a tangential fashion because such data simply are not available for individual faculty members.

A conflict exists between the desire to take account of these factors as one might do in an aggregative occupational study and the desire to take into account the individual productivities and characteristics of particular faculty members. The latter type of study is essentially micro in character and is most successful when it is based upon observations of individual faculty.

At the center of the sex discrimination debate, and affirmative action programs, is the concept of equal pay for equal work. In a cross-sectional context, it is impossible to make even a preliminary determination of whether equal pay for equal work exists if one does not possess reliable measures of individual faculty productivity and performance. On the other hand, it is not absolutely necessary that one possess labor force participation rate data, and so forth, in order to do a cross-sectional study of sex discrimination and affirmative action. Hence, it is preferable, if a choice must be made, to opt for productivity data relating to individual faculty as opposed to doing an aggregative study in which labor force participation rates and the like can be taken into account but individual productivity and performance differentials are for naught. Also, since work, productivity, and evaluation standards differ between campuses, an aggregative study above the institutional or discipline level is not able to address itself adequately to the equal-pay-for-equal-work issue. Only a localized, intensively micro-oriented study can do so. It is for this reason that the empirical work presented in Chapter 5 does not take into account any of the caveats noted in this chapter. The authors are cognizant of the problems involved, but feel strongly that their chosen methodology is far superior when the topic is sex discrimination and affirmative action on an individual rather than an occupational basis.

5

The Empirical Work

Policy squabbles often result because citizens have differing ideas about what is the true state of affairs. These differing ideas can in principle be eliminated by careful empirical work carried out in the spirit of positive economics.

This chapter is devoted to a detailed empirical examination of the operation of an affirmative action salary-increment program for female faculty at Illinois State University. This program was carried out over the space of two academic years (1972-73 and 1973-74).

The *raison d'être* of an affirmative action salary program is the existence of discrimination in salaries against some faculty. The empirical work reported here concentrates upon sex discrimination and affirmative action salary increments given to female faculty. The initial step in the empirical analysis is an examination of whether discrimination against female faculty did exist in the salary structure at Illinois State University prior to the implementation of the affirmative action salary program. Whether or not it did exist, an affirmative action salary-increment program was initiated. Thus, the second step in the analysis is to examine the affirmative action salary program in order to determine what effects, if any, it had upon the faculty salary structure and upon any sex discrimination that might have existed.

The Data Set

The data set consists of individual observations of all full-time, nonadministrative faculty at Illinois State University who held a continuing (nonterminal) contract any of five different academic years, beginning with 1971-72 and ending with 1975-76. Part-time faculty were not included in the data set because their salaries and their responsibilities differ substantially from those of full-time faculty. Further, part-time faculty at Illinois State University are not evaluated in the same fashion as full-time faculty. All academic administrators, whether or not they held academic rank, were eliminated from the data set on the ground that they too have duties, reward structures, and responsibilities substantially different from nonadministrative faculty. The duties of an administrator, for

---

Robert Button, "Positive Economics and Social Policy," Berg Lecture, mimeographed (Normal, Illinois: Illinois State University, 1972). Reprinted with permission.

example, seldom include scholarly publication. Those faculty who held one-year contracts in any given year were also eliminated from the data set because their reward structure, and particularly their duties and responsibilities, differs sharply from those of other faculty.

The number of individual faculty in the data set for each academic year is as follows: 1971-72, $N = 479$; 1972-73, $N = 516$; 1973-74, $N = 559$; 1974-75, $N = 590$; 1975-76, $N = 589$. The data set includes all faculty who met the qualifications cited in the above paragraph. Faculty from all the university's 30+ departments and from all its five colleges are represented in the data set.

The data set is especially interesting because it allows one to observe changes in faculty compensation over time. During the first academic year contained in the data set (1971-72), no affirmative action salary program existed. During the next two academic years (1972-73 and 1973-74), affirmative action salary payments were made to many female faculty members. During the final two academic years encompassed by the data set, no affirmative action salary payments were made. Hence, the data set affords the possibility of "before" and "after" views of the salary structure with respect to the affirmative action program carried out.

The Variables

The variables utilized in the empirical work consist of three major types: (1) salary variables, (2) merit variables, and (3) nonmerit variables. The *salary variables* represent the monthly salary (in dollars) of the faculty member in a given academic year. The *merit variables* reflect the evaluations of each faculty member's performance made by an elected peer group in the faculty member's department. The *nonmerit variables* represent other academic or demographic characteristics known about the faculty member, for example, the faculty member's academic year, the faculty member's age, and so forth.

Salary Variables

Each of the faculty members in the data set possesses a contract which is 9 months in duration. The faculty member's salary is payable over the 9-month period and is quoted at a monthly rate, for example, $2,000 per month. We are interested in the faculty member's salary inclusive of any affirmative action salary increments made (SAL), exclusive of any affirmative action salary increments made ($SAL - AFF$), and in the affirmative action salary increment itself (AFF). The empirical results are grouped in particular academic years; therefore, there is no need to subscript these labels by the academic year involved.

SAL = salary of faculty member in dollars, monthly rate
$SAL - AFF$ = salary of faculty member in dollars, monthly rate, exclusive
                        of any affirmative action salary increments received

AFF   = affirmative action salary increment received by faculty
member in dollars, monthly rate

Merit Variables

The productivity and performance of each Illinois State University faculty
member are evaluated annually in three areas (teaching, scholarly productivity,
and service). The evaluation procedure is carried out by an elected committee of
faculty in each department. Each departmental committee is charged with ranking each of their departmental faculty as exhibiting "inadequate merit," "some
merit," "considerable merit," or "unusual merit" in each of the three performance
categories cited above. Hence, a particular faculty member might be ranked as
being of "considerable merit" in teaching, "some merit" in scholarly productivity,
and "unusual merit" in service.

This type of evaluation system is not uncommon, although it is far from
being ubiquitous. What is rare is that such evaluations have been made available,
albeit without particular faculty names attached, to the authors. No published
studies of faculty salary determination have ever had the benefit of such data
(with the sole exception of the previously published work of the authors). From
an a priori standpoint, peer evaluations are usually preferred to others on the
grounds of evaluator familiarity, particularly when the teaching or service performance of the faculty member is in question. Nationally based studies such as
that carried out by Bayer and Astin[1] have fallen critically short in this context
by being forced to ignore the teaching and service dimensions of faculty performance because of lack of data. It is doubtful, however, that one can make a
reliable judgment about equal pay for equal work without some measure of differential employee productivity.

The authors are cognizant of the possible problems associated with reliance
upon departmental peer evaluations of the productivity and performance of each
faculty member. Not the least among these problems is possible bias (even
though unintentional) exhibited by peer evaluators. We have dealt with this possibility in the previous chapter. The advantages in terms of explanatory power
seem, however, to outweigh the possible deficiencies associated with the use of
peer evaluations.

The peer merit evaluations of teaching performance (*TEA*), scholarly productivity (*SCH*), and service and committee work (*SERV*) are each specified as
a multiple-category dummy variable in the analysis which follows. "Unusual
merit" for each variable is the excluded category. For each variable, the following suffixes apply:

$$I = \begin{cases} 1 & \text{if the faculty member is evaluated as "inadequate"} \\ 0 & \text{otherwise} \end{cases}$$

$$S = \begin{cases} 1 & \text{if the faculty member is evaluated as "some merit"} \\ 0 & \text{otherwise} \end{cases}$$

$$C = \begin{cases} 1 & \text{if the faculty member is evaluated as "considerable merit"} \\ 0 & \text{otherwise} \end{cases}$$

Thus, *TEA - I* refers to the peer merit evaluation of teaching as being Inadequate.

Nonmerit Variables

If the salary structure at Illinois State University were solely shaped and determined by the peer merit evaluations of individual faculty performance, then there would be no need to take into account additional characteristics of individual faculty—for example, the faculty member's race or age. Additionally, holding aside the question of possible bias in the peer evaluations themselves, there would be no sex discrimination. Each faculty member would be paid on the basis of his or her evaluated productivity.

Such is not the case, however. One obvious consideration which causes individual faculty salaries to deviate from those dictated by peer merit evaluations is the influence of the outside market for a particular faculty member's discipline (for example, economics) or even that faculty member's specialty within the discipline (for example, industrial organization). The influence of external market conditions upon the salary of each faculty member is specified as a multiple-category dummy variable with three mutually exclusive classes: strong external market, moderate external market, and weak external market. The strong external market is the excluded category.

$$MKTWEAK = \begin{cases} 1 & \text{if faculty member's discipline and/or specialty is characterized by weak external market demand} \\ 0 & \text{otherwise} \end{cases}$$

$$MKTMOD = \begin{cases} 1 & \text{if faculty member's discipline and/or specialty is characterized by moderate external market demand} \\ 0 & \text{otherwise} \end{cases}$$

The external market conditions were approximated by use of the Caffrey report for the American Council on Education[2] and an interuniversity salary study provided by the Director of Institutional Research at Illinois State University.[a] Since it is absolute salaries that are primarily in question in this study, it

---

[a]The interinstitutional salary survey is carried out by seventeen Midwestern universities, of which Illinois State University is one. It is carried out for the information of the seventeen universities and is not published externally.

is the typical market condition for a discipline over a period of time that is relevant rather than market conditions in the latter half of the 1970's.

Presumably the degree status of a faculty member affects that faculty member's salary. The Ph.D., for example, is often regarded as the "union card" of academia. Possession of the Ph.D. is not explicitly related to a faculty member's salary at Illinois State University, although in the absence of a Ph.D. it is very difficult for a faculty member to advance beyond the assistant-professor rank, and then only in areas of the university where a degree such as Master of Fine Arts is frequently regarded as terminal in nature. While salaries are not tied explicitly to either degree or rank, it is clear that degree and rank are often used as a rationale for salary increments or as a basis for an initial salary offer to a new faculty member. Possession of the Ph.D. is specified as a dummy variable.

$$PHD = \begin{cases} 1 & \text{if faculty member possesses a doctoral degree} \\ 0 & \text{otherwise} \end{cases}$$

Academic rank is also included in the list of regressors. The influence of academic rank upon the salary of each faculty member is specified as a multiple-category dummy variable with full professor being the excluded category.

$$INST = \begin{cases} 1 & \text{if the faculty member is an instructor} \\ 0 & \text{otherwise} \end{cases}$$

$$ASST = \begin{cases} 1 & \text{if the faculty member is an assistant professor} \\ 0 & \text{otherwise} \end{cases}$$

$$ASSO = \begin{cases} 1 & \text{if the faculty member is an associate professor} \\ 0 & \text{otherwise} \end{cases}$$

It has been argued by some that academic rank is: (1) a proxy for merit, and (2) contaminated by sex discrimination.[3] In the first case, the contention is that academic rank and merit variables such as those outlined here are highly collinear. The authors do not believe this to be the case at Illinois State University. Simple correlation coefficients between merit indicators and academic rank are not statistically significant. This probably reflects the fact that Illinois State University has changed rapidly in terms of its size and institutional mission. This has caused promotional standards to be much higher in recent years vis-a-vis former years. For that reason, many faculty who are in the higher academic ranks would not qualify for that rank under the currently applied standards. Consequently, the relationship between merit and academic rank at Illinois State University is weak. With regard to the second contention, one of the authors has performed a factual-counterfactual study of possible sex discrimination in academic ranks at the university. No statistically significant evidence of sex discrimination in academic ranks could be found.[4]

It is conceivable also that the tenure status of a particular faculty member affects that faculty member's salary. Once again, however, this is essentially an empirical question since such a consideration is nowhere stated as a criterion for the reimbursement of faculty at Illinois State University. Tenure status is specified as a dummy variable.

$$TENURE = \begin{cases} 1 & \text{if the faculty member is tenured} \\ 0 & \text{otherwise} \end{cases}$$

The influence of experience is complex. On the one hand, if experience actually results in a more productive employee, then the peer merit evaluations should presumably reflect that fact. In this sense, the authors feel that they do not necessarily need to place such emphasis upon "predegree experience" and "postdegree experience" as have Stafford and Johnson.[5] On the other hand, even when experience does not result in a change in performance or productivity, it might still influence a faculty member's salary. Experience may solidify political connections and friendships, and it may also be used by some decisionmakers as a proxy for performance and productivity. This latter possibility seems to hold true when a salary schedule exists which ties faculty salaries to experience. Such is not the case at Illinois State University. Nonetheless, it seems wise to specify experience variables to determine to what extent experience has an influence upon faculty salaries which is independent of evaluated performance and productivity. The following experience-related variables are utilized.

YEARS   = years that faculty member has possessed a doctorate
YEARSQ = years, squared, that faculty member has possessed a doctorate
YRSR   = years that faculty member has spent in current academic rank
YRSRSQ = years, squared, that faculty member has spent in current academic rank
AGE   = faculty member's age
AGESQ   = faculty member's age, squared

The squared terms on the experience-related variables are specified in order to take account of possible nonlinearities which may characterize the relationship between salary and experience. Johnson and Stafford, for example, argue strongly in favor of this type of specification and further found empirical evidence in support of it.[6]

It addition to sex discrimination, race discrimination may also pervade a faculty salary structure. Both sex and race dummy variables have been specified in this study.

$$SEX \ \ = \begin{cases} 1 & \text{if the faculty member is male} \\ 0 & \text{otherwise} \end{cases}$$

$$RACE = \begin{cases} 1 & \text{if the faculty member is a white, Caucasian (“other} \\ & \text{American”)} \\ 0 & \text{otherwise} \end{cases}$$

Specification

The basic tool of the empirical analysis is multiple regression, which is linear in all parameters. The salary of faculty member i in a given year is made a function of some of or all the j characteristics discussed in the previous section. Equation (5.1) expresses this relationship.

$$SAL_i = a + \Sigma_j \, \beta_j \, (X_{ji}) \qquad (i = 1, 2, \ldots, N \text{ and } j = 1, 2, \therefore ., M) \quad (5.1)$$

where $\quad X_{ji} = $ characteristic j of faculty member i
$\qquad\quad N = $ number of faculty
$\qquad\quad M = $ number of characteristics

A semi-log specification will also be utilized:

$$\ln SAL_i = a + \Sigma_j \, \beta_j \, (X_{ji}) \qquad\qquad\qquad (5.2)$$

Expected Signs on Variables

Assume a relationship of the form specified in Equation (5.1). The expected sign on the partial regression coefficient of each of the ordinal peer merit evaluation categories is *negative* because "unusual merit" is the excluded category. From an a priori standpoint, a "some merit" ranking should result in a "penalty" being assessed the faculty member. The penalty is the number of dollars that the faculty member does not receive because he or she has been ranked below the excluded category, "unusual merit." The penalties should become increasingly large (in an absolute-value sense) as the merit evaluation becomes increasingly low. The largest penalty (the smallest number when the negative sign is taken into consideration) should be assessed someone who is assigned an "inadequate" rating by the peer evaluators.

The external market variable is once again a multiple-category dummy variable where the excluded category is the strongest market. Hence, the expected sign on the partial regression coefficients of the market variables is negative, and increasingly large penalties should be imposed upon increasingly weaker external market situations.

The influences of the possession of the doctorate and the holding of tenure on the part of a faculty member are expected to be positive. The effects of experience-related variables (*YEARS*, *YEARSQ*, *YRSR*, *YRSRSQ*, *AGE*, and *AGESQ*) upon salary are not clear from an a priori standpoint. Experience may increase the specificity of human capital and make the faculty member more productive. On the other hand, experience and age may, after a certain point, result in the faculty member becoming out of date with respect to developments in his or her discipline. The quadratic terms may conceivably reflect this. It is an empirical question whether or not some older, more experienced faculty members are "over the hill." Hence, the expected sign is unclear with respect to either the linear or the quadratic terms.

Discrimination, particularly sex discrimination, is the centerpiece of this study. If sex discrimination against female faculty exists, then a positive sign should appear on the partial regression coefficient of the *SEX* variable. If race discrimination against nonwhite, non-Caucasian faculty exists, then a positive sign is the expectation for the partial regression coefficient of the *RACE* variable.

The Existence of Sex Discrimination

Two different methods will be used to determine to what extent sex discrimination against female faculty in absolute salaries existed at Illinois State University. The first approach inserts a sex dummy variable directly into a salary-estimating equation. The sign and size of the partial regression coefficient on this variable, and statistical significance of the coefficient, lead to a judgment about the presence or absence of mean sex discrimination against female faculty as a class. The second approach relies upon a factual-counterfactual methodology. A salary-estimating equation for male faculty only is obtained; the regression coefficients from this equation are then used to generate a counterfactual estimate of what female faculty would be paid if they were compensated in accordance with the determinants of male faculty salaries. That is, the counterfactual estimate results when the determinants of male faculty salaries (exclusive of sex) are applied to female faculty.

The Sex Dummy Variable Approach

Tables 5-1 through 5-7 report the results of multiple regressions which seek to ascertain the determinants of faculty salaries in five different academic years, beginning with 1971-72 and ending with 1975-76. The partial regression coefficient on the *SEX* variable in Table 5-1 is 50.55. This implies that a mean tax of $50.55 per month was placed upon femaleness (*ceteris paribus*). This coefficient is statistically significant at the 0.05 level and relates to the 1971-72 academic year.

An affirmative action salary increment program for female faculty was

Table 5-1
Determinants of Monthly Salaries of 479 Faculty, 1971-72

Dependent Variable: Monthly Salary in Dollars of 479 Faculty
Constant: 1,180.4

R^2: 0.705   *SEE: 191.4*   *F: 45.2*[a]

Independent Variable	Partial Regression Coefficient	Standard Error	Level of Significance[b]
TEA1	99.24	219.76	0.65
TEA2	− 32.30	29.24	0.27
TEA3	4.05	23.37	0.86
SCH1	37.21	64.14	0.56
SCH2	− 10.55	28.50	0.71
SCH3	17.00	28.20	0.54
SERV1	−285.27	107.08	0.00
SERV2	− 30.72	27.67	0.26
SERV3	− 25.33	24.69	0.30
INST	−628.30	66.22	0.00
ASST	−408.44	48.54	0.00
ASSO	−283.75	33.34	0.00
MKTLOW	− 83.15	57.27	0.14
MKTMED	− 79.18	56.65	0.16
AGE	25.57	10.36	0.01
AGESQ	− 0.28	0.12	0.01
YEARS	11.10	6.58	0.09
YEARSQ	− 0.23	0.23	0.32
YRSR	21.96	4.18	0.00
YRSRSQ	− 0.63	0.08	0.00
PHD	138.90	29.75	0.00
TENURE	15.06	26.77	0.57
RACE	14.32	46.09	0.75
SEX	50.55	22.73	0.02

[a]Statistically significant at the 0.01 level.

[b]One-tailed test.

initiated in the 1972-73 academic year. Prior to the dispensation of the affirmative action salary increments (but after the regular salary increments had been received by all faculty, including women), mean sex discrimination against female faculty had risen to $66.69 per month. This estimate is the partial regression coefficient of the *SEX* variable in Table 5-2 and is statistically significant at the 0.01 level.

Table 5-3 reports the determinants of faculty salaries *after* the affirmative action salary increments were dispensed in the 1972-73 academic year. The partial regression coefficient of the *SEX* variable has fallen to 49.55, and is still

Table 5-2

Determinants of Monthly Salaries of 516 Faculty, Prior to Any Affirmative Action Payment, 1972–73

Dependent Variable: Monthly Salary in Dollars of 516 Faculty

Constant: 3,112.4

R^2: 0.856   *SEE: 124.8*   *F: 121.2*[a]

Independent Variable	Partial Regression Coefficient	Standard Error	Level of Significance[b]
TEA1	118.59	77.64	0.12
TEA2	− 61.61	17.26	0.00
TEA3	− 31.21	14.58	0.03
SCH1	−102.52	38.62	0.00
SCH2	− 56.53	19.29	0.00
SCH3	− 17.94	18.30	0.32
SERV1	−221.88	57.76	0.00
SERV2	− 71.95	16.76	0.00
SERV3	− 46.96	15.34	0.00
INST	−611.87	42.45	0.00
ASST	−410.34	29.50	0.00
ASSO	−246.62	20.08	0.00
MKTLOW	−163.29	27.55	0.00
MKTMED	−127.83	27.29	0.00
AGE	29.15	5.80	0.00
AGESQ	− 0.30	0.06	0.00
YEARS	13.62	3.00	0.00
YEARSQ	− 0.26	0.06	0.00
YRSR	32.52	4.77	0.00
YRSRSQ	− 1.21	0.27	0.00
PHD	80.03	19.19	0.00
TENURE	− 33.57	16.41	0.04
RACE	− 16.14	28.17	0.56
SEX	66.69	14.64	0.00

[a]Statistically significant at the 0.01 level

[b]One-tailed test

statistically significant at the 0.01 level. The first year of the affirmative action salary-increment program therefore reduced the mean estimate of sex discrimination by $66.09 – $49.55 = $16.54 per month per faculty member.

The second phase of the affirmative action salary-increment program took place in the 1973-74 academic year. After regular salary increments had been dispensed, but *before* affirmative action salary increments were distributed, the mean estimate of sex discrimination had fallen to $24.58 per month per female faculty member. This partial regression coefficient relates to the *SEX* variable in Table 5-4 and is statistically significant at the 0.10 level. The fact that the

Table 5-3
Determinants of Monthly Salaries of 516 Faculty, after Affirmative Action Payments, 1972-73

Dependent Variable: *Monthly Salary in Dollars of 516 Faculty*
Constant: *1,311.3*

R^2: *0.857*   *SEE: 123.5*   *F: 122.9*[a]

Independent Variable	Partial Regression Coefficient	Standard Error	Level of Significance[b]
TEA1	121.53	76.83	0.11
TEA2	− 60.74	17.09	0.00
TEA3	− 30.08	14.43	0.03
SCH1	−103.75	38.21	0.00
SCH2	− 54.90	19.09	0.00
SCH3	− 15.02	18.11	0.40
SERV1	−222.70	57.16	0.00
SERV2	− 71.19	16.59	0.00
SERV3	− 47.41	15.18	0.00
INST	−619.27	42.01	0.00
ASST	−412.59	29.19	0.00
ASSO	−246.08	19.87	0.00
MKTLOW	−164.59	27.26	0.00
MKTMED	−131.99	27.00	0.00
AGE	29.49	5.74	0.00
AGESQ	− 0.30	0.06	0.00
YEARS	13.74	2.97	0.00
YEARSQ	− 0.26	0.06	0.00
YRSR	32.18	4.72	0.00
YRSRSQ	− 1.19	0.27	0.00
PHD	78.73	18.99	0.00
TENURE	− 32.07	16.24	0.04
RACE	− 18.33	27.88	0.51
SEX	49.55	14.49	0.00

[a]Statistically significant at the 0.01 level

[b]One-tailed test

mean estimate of sex discrimination fell by $49.55 - $24.58 = $24.97 per month *without* any affirmative action can be variously interpreted. One attractive hypothesis is that decisionmakers and evaluators took great pains to avoid possible sex discrimination in salary increments and the $24.97 per month reflects this. An alternative paradigm is that decisionmakers and evaluators were intimidated into doing so. Whatever the case, the mean estimate of sex discrimination was halved during the regular salary-increment process without resorting to affirmative action.

The affirmative action salary increments which actually were dispensed in

Table 5-4

Determinants of Monthly Salaries of 559 Faculty, prior to Any Affirmative Action Payment, 1973-74

Dependent Variable: Monthly Salary in Dollars of 559 Faculty
Constant: 1,601.7

R^2: 0.772   *SEE: 157.1*   *F: 75.2*[a]

Independent Variable	Partial Regression Coefficient	Standard Error	Level of Significance[b]
TEA1	− 66.19	104.43	0.52
TEA2	− 86.89	22.46	0.00
TEA3	− 59.55	16.90	0.00
SCH1	−121.58	38.20	0.00
SCH2	− 45.67	20.51	0.02
SCH3	− 21.20	18.73	0.25
SERV1	− 14.16	57.57	0.80
SERV2	− 24.45	19.78	0.21
SERV3	− 21.35	17.39	0.22
INST	−584.99	52.43	0.00
ASST	−389.80	31.91	0.00
ASSO	−214.80	22.38	0.00
MKTLOW	−131.87	32.03	0.00
MKTMED	− 99.74	32.07	0.00
AGE	17.38	8.26	0.03
AGESQ	− 0.16	0.09	0.07
YEARS	21.19	5.18	0.00
YEARSQ	− 0.42	0.16	0.01
YRSR	22.33	5.32	0.00
YRSRSQ	− 0.76	0.30	0.01
PHD	31.73	27.63	0.25
TENURE	− 2.79	21.15	0.89
RACE	− 59.72	33.69	0.07
SEX	24.58	17.30	0.15

[a]Statistically significant at the 0.01 level

[b]One-tailed test

the 1973-74 academic year resulted in the erasure of mean discrimination against female faculty according to Table 5-5. The partial regression coefficient on the *SEX* variable changed sign and was statistically insignificant even at the 0.50 level.

No affirmative action salary program was undertaken in the 1974-75 academic year. Table 5-6 reports the determinants of faculty salaries in that year. The partial regression coefficient on the *SEX* variable rose to 6.26, but was not statistically significant even at the 0.70 level. Extrapolations concerning regression coefficients which are not statistically significant are hazardous and unreliable.

Table 5-5
Determinants of Monthly Salaries of 559 Faculty, after Affirmative Action Payments, 1973-74

Dependent Variable: Monthly Salary in Dollars of 559 Faculty
Constant: 1,693.4

R^2: 0.772   *SEE: 155.0*   *F: 75.3*[a]

Independent Variable	Partial Regression Coefficient	Standard Error	Level of Significance[b]
TEA1	− 84.03	103.01	0.41
TEA2	− 86.03	22.15	0.00
TEA3	− 59.07	16.67	0.00
SCH1	−119.23	37.68	0.00
SCH2	− 42.18	20.23	0.03
SCH3	− 26.30	18.47	0.15
SERV1	− 12.62	56.78	0.82
SERV2	− 25.45	19.51	0.19
SERV3	− 22.10	17.15	0.19
INST	−590.20	51.72	0.00
ASST	−383.56	31.48	0.00
ASSO	−217.08	22.08	0.00
MKTLOW	−127.20	31.60	0.00
MKTMED	− 97.92	31.64	0.00
ACE	14.78	8.15	0.07
AGESQ	− 0.13	0.09	0.15
YEARS	22.43	5.10	0.00
YEARSQ	− 0.47	0.16	0.00
YRSR	19.94	5.24	0.00
YRSRSQ	− 0.72	0.29	0.01
PHD	25.51	27.25	0.35
TENURE	− 0.83	20.86	0.96
RACE	− 66.61	33.23	0.04
SEX	− 9.63	17.07	0.57

[a]Statistically significant at the 0.01 level

[b]One-tailed test

Nonetheless, one might view the reappearance of a positive partial regression coefficient on the *SEX* variable as evidence of attempts of decisionmakers and evaluators to counteract the effects of affirmative action salary increments in the previous two years. It is impossible to test this hypothesis directly with the data set available.

Table 5-7 reveals that the partial regression coefficient on the *SEX* variable remained fairly constant between the 1974-75 and 1975-76 academic years. In 1974-75, the coefficient was 6.76, whereas it was 15.09 in 1975-76. Neither coefficient was statistically significant at conventional levels.

Table 5-6
Determinants of Monthly Salaries of 590 Faculty, 1974-75

Dependent Variable: Monthly Salary in Dollars of 590 Faculty
Constant: 1,728.9

R^2: 0.742   *SEE: 197.0*   *F: 67.7*[a]

Independent Variable	Partial Regression Coefficient	Standard Error	Level of Significance[b]
TEA1	− 57.49	87.69	0.51
TEA2	−107.95	30.51	0.00
TEA3	− 39.40	18.96	0.03
SCH1	1.71	40.15	0.96
SCH2	− 72.32	25.60	0.00
SCH3	− 36.01	22.32	0.10
SERV1	−587.69	94.59	0.00
SERV2	− 61.32	24.42	0.01
SERV3	− 3.52	19.81	0.85
INST	−774.41	70.19	0.00
ASST	−546.49	42.56	0.00
ASSO	−283.99	27.73	0.00
MKTLOW	−187.80	37.25	0.00
MKTMED	−143.00	36.94	0.00
AGE	19.51	9.52	0.04
AGESQ	− 0.18	0.10	0.07
YEARS	15.51	5.98	0.01
YEARSQ	− 0.47	0.18	0.01
YRSR	31.26	3.50	0.00
YRSRSQ	− 0.71	0.06	0.00
PHD	19.98	34.73	0.56
TENURE	− 0.01	26.04	1.00
RACE	22.00	38.60	0.56
SEX	6.26	20.73	0.76

[a]Statistically significant at the 0.01 level

[b]One-tailed test

We will parenthetically note one startling result in Table 5-7 which has implications for affirmative action programs in other arenas related to race discrimination. The partial regression coefficient on the *RACE* variable was −154.11
and was statistically significant at the 0.01 level. This implies mean discrimination of $154.11 per month per faculty member in *favor* of nonwhite, non-Caucasian
faculty members. It would be risky to make too much of this, however. A review of Tables 5-1 through 5-7 reveals that in two of the seven cases, the partial
regression coefficient of the *RACE* variable was positive in sign. The number of
nonwhite, non-Caucasian faculty members involved was only 32 in the 1975-76
academic year. This may cause estimation problems, particularly in the presence

Table 5-7

Determinants of Monthly Salaries of 589 Faculty, 1975-76

Dependent Variable: *Monthly Salary in Dollars of 589 Faculty*

Constant: *1,794.6*

R^2:   *0.730*   *SEE: 205.4*   *F: 66.6*[a]

Independent Variable	Partial Regression Coefficient	Standard Error	Level of Significance[b]
TEA2	− 0.22	34.57	0.99
TEA3	− 43.22	19.85	0.03
SCH1	75.39	52.13	0.14
SCH2	− 44.23	26.12	0.09
SCH3	− 19.51	23.37	0.40
SERV1	−131.40	85.34	0.12
SERV2	− 24.18	28.06	0.38
SERV3	− 3.12	20.31	0.87
INST	−964.86	82.66	0.00
ASST	−623.42	42.22	0.00
ASSO	−333.73	28.44	0.00
MKTLOW	−171.15	53.49	0.00
MKTMED	−147.17	52.87	0.00
AGE	32.12	10.77	0.00
AGESQ	− 0.33	0.11	0.00
YEARS	15.01	6.50	0.02
YEARSQ	− 0.29	0.19	0.13
YRSR	44.16	6.00	0.00
YRSRSQ	− 1.45	0.30	0.00
PHD	− 16.95	39.60	0.66
TENURE	− 91.11	27.61	0.00
RACE	−154.11	38.70	0.00
SEX	15.09	22.52	0.50

[a]Statistically significant at the 0.01 level

[b]One-tailed test

of multicollinearity among independent variables. We will deal with the multi-collinearity issue shortly.

The Factual-Counterfactual Approach

A factual-counterfactual approach to sex discrimination is preferable to a dummy-variable approach on two counts. First, as we have seen, the factual-counterfactual approach most closely corresponds to the requirements of the law. Second, the econometric grounding of counterfactualism is superior. The dummy-variable approach yields an estimate of the effect of sex upon salaries, with all other variables held constant. This can be interpreted as a measure of the parallel shift that takes place in the regression line due to sex. That is, only the constant term is affected. The factual-counterfactual approach, on the other hand, allows sex to affect the entire regression structure instead of only the constant. All independent variables are allowed to vary in response to sex. Hence, counterfactualism yields a superior estimate of the degree and amount of sex discrimination.

The affirmative action salary-increment program at Illinois State University was carried over a two-year time period, and our factual-counterfactual analysis will take account of that time sequence.

1972-73. The first step in the factual-counterfactual methodology where sex discrimination is concerned is to estimate a salary equation for one sex only. Either one can estimate a salary equation for male faculty and then apply these estimated coefficients to female faculty, or one can estimate a salary equation for female faculty and then apply these estimated coefficients to male faculty. We will present results from both approaches. The estimation of a salary equation for male faculty, however, seems to be more appropriate for our purposes since it is sex discrimination against female faculty that is our major concern. We will therefore emphasize this approach, although not to the exclusion of the other.

Table 5-8 records the determinants of the salaries of 399 male faculty in the 1972-73 academic year. The coefficient of determination (0.835) is high in light of the cross-sectional nature of the data set, and many of the partial regression coefficients are statistically significant at the 0.01 level. The expected signs of the partial regression coefficients are generally realized. It should be noted that all the linear experience variables (*YRSR, YEARS,* and *AGE*) have positive coefficients which are statistically significant at the 0.01 level. By way of contrast, the quadratic experience variables (*YRSRSQ, YEARSQ,* and *AGESQ*) have negative coefficients which are statistically significant at the 0.01 level. This supports the validity of the supposition that there is a nonlinear relationship between salary and experience-related variables. In the case at hand, additional experience increases male faculty salaries, but at a decreasing rate. That is, diminishing returns exist with respect to incremental experience for male faculty.

The estimated coefficients reported in Table 5-8 were then utilized to generate a counterfactual salary for each female faculty member. Depending upon the individual female faculty member's characteristics, dollar amounts (based upon the coefficients in Table 5-8) were subtracted from the constant 1,116.2, also found in Table 5-8. For example, $578.36 was subtracted from the constant when the female faculty member in question held the academic rank of instructor; $76.13 was added if that faculty member possessed a doctorate. A similar process was followed for each of the 23 independent variables. The

Table 5-8
Determinants of Monthly Salaries of 399 Male Faculty, 1972-73

Dependent Variable: Monthly Salary in Dollars of 399 Male Faculty
Constant: 1,116.2

R^2: 0.835   *SEE: 128.7*   *F: 82.4*[a]

Independent Variable	Partial Regression Coefficient	Standard Error	Level of Significance[b]
TEA1	152.40	83.56	0.06
TEA2	− 57.21	20.33	0.00
TEA3	− 24.59	17.61	0.16
SCH1	− 82.18	46.39	0.07
SCH2	− 46.24	22.97	0.04
SCH3	− 3.58	21.11	0.86
SERV1	−295.00	86.03	0.00
SERV2	− 72.79	19.75	0.00
SERV3	− 51.73	17.87	0.00
INST	−578.36	54.89	0.00
ASST	−404.97	33.14	0.00
ASSO	−244.84	22.44	0.00
MKTLOW	−165.72	29.68	0.00
MKTMED	−133.08	29.25	0.00
AGE	37.80	7.62	0.00
AGESQ	− 0.39	0.08	0.00
YEARS	15.12	3.43	0.00
YEARSQ	− 0.27	0.07	0.00
YRSR	34.84	6.41	0.00
YRSRSQ	− 1.19	0.33	0.00
PHD	76.13	22.64	0.00
TENURE	− 39.27	19.38	0.04
RACE	− 18.67	35.02	0.59

[a]Statistically significant at the 0.01 level

[b]One-tailed test

sum of the constant plus these additions and subtractions is the counterfactual estimate of what the female faculty member in question would have earned had she been paid according to the same determinants as male faculty.

The application of the factual-counterfactual model to the 1972-73 academic year revealed that 94 of the 117 female faculty (80 percent) had actual monthly salaries (Y_A) less than their counterfactual monthly salaries (Y_{CF}) prior to any affirmative action salary increments. The difference between the faculty member's actual salary and her counterfactual salary is termed the "counterfactual residual" and is equal to $Y_A - Y_{CF}$.

Table 5-9 records both the counterfactual residual and the affirmative action

Table 5-9
The Number of Female Faculty by Size of Residual and Affirmative Action Payment, 1972-73

Affirmative Action Payment (dollars per month)	Residuals = Actual Monthly Salary − Counterfactual Salary = $Y_A - Y_{CF}$								Totals
	−201 or less	−151 to −200	−101 to −150	−51 to −100	−1 to −50	0 to 50	51 to 100	101 or more	
0	2	3	6	10	12	10	4	4	51
1-25	7	4	4	9	13	2	1	1	41
26-50	3	3	3	5	2	1	0	0	17
51-75	0	2	3	0	0	0	0	0	5
76-100	1	1	0	0	0	0	0	0	2
101-150	1	0	0	0	0	0	0	0	1
151-250	0	0	0	0	0	0	0	0	0
Totals	14	13	16	24	27	13	5	5	117

Note: The mean residual was −$65 per month; the mean affirmative action salary increment was $29 per month for those female faculty who received payments and $16 per month for all female faculty.

salary increments made to female faculty in the 1972-73 academic year. The mean counterfactual residual for the 117 female faculty was -$65 per month, and was statistically significant at the 0.01 level. The -$65 per month residual implies mean sex discrimination against female faculty by that amount.

The 1972-73 academic year was the first of two years in which affirmative action salary increments were dispensed. The mean affirmative action salary increment received by all female faculty overall was only $16 per month. Only 66 female faculty received such payments, however. The mean payment to these 66 female faculty was $29 per month.

Of the 94 female faculty who were found to have negative counterfactual residuals, only 61 (65 percent) received affirmative action salary increments. Additionally, Table 5-10 indicates that 5 of the 23 female faculty (22 percent) who were found to have positive counterfactual residuals also received affirmative action payments. By the factual-counterfactual criterion, these payments were unnecessary.

While modest in size, the increments dispensed to female faculty in the first year of the affirmative action salary program went predominantly to those female faculty who were underpaid in light of the factual-counterfactual criterion. The simple correlation between the size of the counterfactual residual and the size of the affirmative action salary increment was 0.36. This is

Table 5-10
Salary Discrimination and the Affirmative Action Status of 117 Women Faculty, 1972-73

Circumstance	Number and Percent of Female Faculty	
(1) Salary Discrimination *against* Female Faculty	94	(65%)
Affirmative action salary increments		
Eliminated this discrimination	5	(5%)
Reduced this discrimination	56	(60%)
Increased this discrimination	0	(0%)
Left this discrimination unchanged	33	(35%)
	94	
(2) Salary Discrimination *in favor of* Female Faculty		
Affirmative action salary increments		
Eliminated this discrimination	0	(0%)
Reduced this discrimination	0	(0%)
Increased this discrimination	5	(22%)
Left this discrimination unchanged	18	(78%)
	23	
Total Female Faculty	117	(100%)

statistically significant at the 0.01 level. In this sense, then, the affirmative action salary increment program seems to have proceeded broadly in the direction that the law requires.

The mean characteristics of the group of 66 female faculty who received affirmative action salary increments in the 1972-73 academic year are worthy of note. It can be seen in Table 5-11 that the mean counterfactual residual of this group was -$94 per month. Additionally, however, Table 5-11 records that the 66 recipients were (relative to male faculty): (1) concentrated in lower academic ranks; (2) much less likely to possess a doctorate; (3) somewhat less likely to receive one of the two highest peer merit evaluations of their scholarly productivity; (4) much more likely to be a member of an academic discipline or specialty characterized by excess supply of personnel and a generally tepid market; (5) less experienced in terms of years possessed terminal degree; and (6) about 5 years older in mean age.

The female faculty who exhibited these six characteristics were disproportionately the targets of discriminatory impulses according to the factual-counterfactual model. This finding is consistent with the specific human-capital hypothesis of Landes and others (see Chapter 3). It is also consistent with the wage-discriminating monopsonist model developed in Chapter 3. It seems reasonable to assume that older faculty who labor in excess-supply disciplines and do not possess the doctorate will also have lower wage elasticities of supply for their own labor. Hence, the wage-discriminating monopsonist, in this case Illinois State University, paid these faculty lower wages. This result is cost-minimizing and economically efficient from the standpoint of high-level university administrators who are charged with managing finite budget dollars. Economic efficiency aside, this type of behavior is also sex-discriminatory in the context of the factual-counterfactual model developed here. This latter statement implies that one or more pieces of federal law (especially the Equal Pay Act of 1963) were being violated by this type of salary behavior.

It should be noted parenthetically that possible sex differentials in labor force participation rates, quit rates, and expected future productivity are not taken into account in the previous analysis. What the factual-counterfactual model (and the law) label sex discrimination might therefore disappear in whole or in part if such factors were taken into account. This caveat, however, should function as a flag of caution rather than as a rationale for discounting the entirety of the previous empirical results.

1973-74. The second, and quantitatively most important, affirmative action year was the 1973-74 academic year. For the sample of faculty involved, $1,872 per month was distributed in affirmative action salary payments in the first

Table 5-11
Mean Characteristics of Three Groups of Faculty, 1972-73

Variable	399 Male Faculty	66 Women Faculty Who Received Affirmative Action Money	51 Women Faculty Who Did Not Receive Affirmative Action Money
Academic Rank			
Instructor	3%	10%	21%
Assistant Professor	44%	58%	47%
Associate Professor	31%	14%	16%
Professor	22%	18%	16%
Ph.D.	71%	41%	47%
Teaching Ranking			
Inadequate	1%	0%	0%
Some Merit	32%	23%	27%
Considerable Merit	42%	48%	41%
Unusual Merit	25%	29%	31%
Scholarly Productivity Ranking			
Inadequate	3%	2%	5%
Somer Merit	48%	62%	59%
Considerable Merit	33%	30%	20%
Unusual Merit	16%	6%	16%
Service Ranking			
Inadequate	1%	5%	2%
Some Merit	38%	42%	51%
Considerable Merit	35%	32%	25%
Unusual Merit	26%	21%	22%
Market			
Low	46%	73%	55%
Moderate	48%	26%	45%
High	6%		0%
Race (% Caucasian)	96%	97%	90%
Years since Degree	5.91	3.61	4.05
Age	41	46	44
Salary before Affirmative Action	$1,678	$1,453	$1,526
Counterfactual Residual	0	−$94	−$27

affirmative action year (1972-73). That figure rose to $4,810 per month in the second and final affirmative action year (1973-74). It is of interest to note that the number of female faculty members receiving affirmative action payments decreased from 66 to 53 in the two years.

The counterfactual estimates of female faculty salaries in the 1973-74 academic year were once again generated by making use of a regression of faculty characteristics (excluding sex) upon male faculty salaries. Those results are reported in Table 5-12, which is analogous to Table 5-8 for the previous affirmative action year. Once again, the coefficient of determination is relatively high for cross-sectional data (0.727), the F statistic for the equation as a whole

Table 5-12
Determinants of Monthly Salaries of 429 Male Faculty 1973-74

Dependent Variable: Monthly Salary in Dollars of 429 Faculty
Constant: 1,648.1

R^2: 0.727	SEE: 170.8	F: 46.8[a]	
Independent Variable	Partial Regression Coefficient	Standard Error	Levels of Significance[b]
TEA1	− 66.82	132.29	0.61
TEA2	−100.91	27.69	0.00
TEA3	− 64.14	20.73	0.00
SCH1	−130.65	51.58	0.01
SCH2	− 42.48	24.70	0.08
SCH3	− 29.09	22.39	0.19
SERV1	− 6.03	67.54	0.92
SERV2	− 16.42	24.14	0.49
SERV3	− 16.43	21.77	0.45
INST	−553.63	73.77	0.00
ASST	−368.37	37.88	0.00
ASSO	−210.78	26.00	0.00
MKTLOW	−128.40	35.94	0.00
MKTMED	− 97.04	35.90	0.00
AGE	17.77	11.39	0.12
AGESQ	− 0.17	0.13	0.18
YEARS	24.27	6.23	0.00
YEARSQ	− 0.50	0.20	0.01
YRSR	17.75	6.84	0.01
YRSRSQ	− 0.58	0.38	0.12
PHD	12.53	34.22	0.71
TENURE	12.74	36.60	0.63
RACE	− 99.34	43.72	0.02

[a]Statistically significant at the 0.01 level

[b]One-tailed test

is statistically significant at the 0.01 level, the coefficients assume expected signs, and the coefficients are generally statistically significant at conventional levels.

The relationship between the counterfactual residual $(Y_A - Y_{CF})$ for each female faculty member and the affirmative action salary increment (if any) for each female faculty member is reported in Table 5-13. These results are summarized, by category, in Table 5-14. Of the 130 female faculty in the data set 53 received an affirmative action salary increment which averaged $92 per month. Table 5-13 reveals, however, that the factual-counterfactual methodology uncovered evidence of sex discrimination against female faculty in 87 of the 130 cases. Nonetheless, despite the fact that a significant proportion of female faculty who were discriminated against did not receive affirmative action monies (Table 5-14 reveals that 46 percent of those discriminated against did not receive any affirmative action salary increment), *mean* discrimination against female faculty *as a class* was eliminated by the affirmative action salary increments. This follows from the fact that the mean counterfactual residual for all female faculty was –$30 per month prior to the increments, and the mean affirmative action payment made to all female faculty (recipients and nonrecipients alike) was $37 per month.

One must be careful in stating that mean class discrimination against female faculty was eliminated by the affirmative action salary program. First, a difference-of-means test revealed that the $30 difference between the actual and counterfactual salaries of female faculty was not statistically significant at the 0.10 level. Hence, one cannot rigorously argue that such discrimination existed in the first instance. A second factor to be taken into account is that the elimination of discrimination in faculty salaries against female faculty as a class does not imply that the same was true for all or even most individual female faculty. Indeed, Table 5-14 indicates that 67 of the 87 female faculty who had negative counterfactual residuals *before* the affirmative action salary increments also had negative counterfactual residuals after the increments had been dispensed.

What were the characteristics of female faculty who received affirmative action salary increments in the 1973-74 academic year? Table 5-15 virtually reiterates the characteristics found in the 1972-73 academic year. The 58 female faculty who received affirmative action salary payments in the 1973-74 academic year were, relative to male faculty, generally: (1) of lower academic rank; (2) recipients of slightly lower peer merit evaluations of their teaching performance; (3) recipients of noticeably lower peer merit evaluations of their scholarly productivity; (4) disproportionately found in low market demand disciplines and specialties; (5) 5 years older in mean age; and (6) in possession of the doctorate 2.63 years less.

A glance at Table 5-15 also reveals, however, that the differences between the 58 women who received affirmative action monies and the 77 women who did not, are less noticeable. Indeed, the group of female faculty who did not

Table 5-13
The Number of Female Faculty by Size of Residual and Affirmative Action Payment, 1973-74

Affirmative Action Payment (dollars per month)	Residuals $= Actual\ Monthly\ Salary - Counterfactual\ Salary = Y_A - Y_{CF}$								Totals
	-201 or less	-151 to -200	-101 to -150	-51 to -100	-1 to -50	0 to 50	51 to 100	101 or more	
0	0	1	7	11	21	14	12	11	77
1-25	1	0	0	2	2	1	2	0	8
26-50	0	1	0	5	1	0	0	0	7
51-75	0	2	2	0	3	0	0	0	7
76-100	1	0	4	7	3	0	0	1	16
101-150	1	1	2	2	1	1	0	1	9
151-250	4	1	0	1	0	0	0	0	6
Totals	7	6	15	28	31	16	14	13	130

Note: The mean residual was -$30 per month; the mean affirmative action salary increment was $92 per month for those women faculty who received payments and $37 per month for all women faculty.

Table 5-14
Salary Discrimination and the Affirmative Action Status of 130 Women Faculty, 1973-74

Circumstance	Number and Percent of Female Faculty	
(1) Salary Discrimination		
against Female Faculty	87	(67%)
Affirmative action salary increments		
Eliminated this discrimination	20	(23%)
Reduced this discrimination	27	(31%)
Increased this discrimination	0	(0%)
Left this discrimination unchanged	40	(46%)
	87	
(2) Salary Discrimination		
in favor of Female Faculty	43	(33%)
Affirmative action salary increments		
Eliminated this discrimination	0	(0%)
Reduced this discrimination	0	(0%)
Increased this discrimination	6	(14%)
Left this discrimination unchanged	37	(86%)
	43	
Total Female Faculty	130	(100%)

receive affirmative action salary increments seems often to lie between male faculty and female affirmative action recipients in terms of their characteristics. The major difference between the recipient and nonrecipient groups of female faculty seems to have been the sign and magnitude of the counterfactual residual. The 58 female faculty who received affirmative action salary payments had a mean counterfactual residual of -$87 prior to affirmative action, while the 77 female faculty who did not receive such payments had a mean counterfactual residual of +$9.

It is true that the affirmative action decisionmakers made no use whatsoever of the factual-counterfactual methodology utilized in this study. At the same time, the affirmative action salary increments dispensed in the 1973-74 academic year do bear a relationship to the counterfactual residuals. The simple correlation between the affirmative action salary increments and the counterfactual residuals for each individual was 0.48. This is statistically significant at the 0.01 level. One cannot be too euphoric about this result, however. Only 23 percent of the variance in affirmative action salary payments can be explained by means of the counterfactual residuals.

The focus of our attention is narrowed in Table 5-16 to the 58 female faculty who received affirmative action salary increments. Table 5-16 reports the results of a regression of the size of that increment upon the usual variables in the model.

Table 5-15
Mean Characteristics of Three Groups of Faculty, 1973-74

Variable	429 Male Faculty	58 Women Faculty Who Received Affirmative Action Money	77 Women Faculty Who Did Not Receive Affirmative Action Money
Academic Rank			
Instructor	2%	12%	10%
Assistant Professor	41%	60%	52%
Associate Professor	31%	11%	19%
Professor	26%	17%	19%
Ph.D.	72%	42%	47%
Teaching Ranking			
Inadequate	0%	0%	1%
Some Merit	19%	28%	18%
Considerable Merit	46%	40%	45%
Unusual Merit	35%	32%	36%
Scholarly Productivity Ranking			
Inadequate	4%	11%	9%
Some Merit	36%	51%	34%
Considerable Merit	36%	25%	44%
Unusual Merit	24%	13%	13%
Service Ranking			
Inadequate	2%	2%	1%
Some Merit	32%	32%	25%
Considerable Merit	35%	42%	43%
Unusual Merit	31%	24%	31%
Market			
Low	50%	68%	58%
Moderate	44%	30%	42%
High	6%	2%	0%
Race (% Caucasian)	96%	91%	97%
Age	42	47	45
Years since Degree	6.35	3.62	4.09
Salary before Affirmative Action	$1,745	$1,511	$1,646
Counterfactual Residual	0	-$87	+$9

Table 5-16
Determinants of Positive Affirmative Action Payments Received by 58 Female Faculty, 1973-74

Dependent Variable:	Positive Affirmative Action Salary Increments Received by 58 Female Faculty, 1973–74		
Constant: 38.5			

R^2: 0.460	SEE: 51.8	F: 1.2	
Independent Variable	Partial Regression Coefficient	Standard Error	Level of Significance[a]
TEA2	− 2.52	36.57	0.94
TEA3	11.06	22.34	0.62
SCH1	51.76	49.29	0.30
SCH2	11.27	28.08	0.69
SCH3	− 5.73	29.27	0.84
SERV1	− 46.02	67.96	0.50
SERV2	− 21.50	30.29	0.48
SERV3	− 22.21	26.63	0.41
INST	− 65.14	86.06	0.45
ASST	− 31.49	65.85	0.63
ASSO	− 9.13	47.80	0.85
MKTLOW	111.24	70.32	0.12
MKTMED	89.10	69.36	0.20
AGE	− 0.13	11.00	0.99
AGESQ	0.00	0.12	0.98
YEARS	− 3.44	8.28	0.68
YEARSQ	0.12	0.26	0.64
YRSR	− 12.10	6.38	0.06
YRSRSQ	0.37	0.32	0.25
PHD	− 10.47	35.59	0.77
TENURE	25.45	27.72	0.36
RACE	19.41	27.81	0.49

[a]One-tailed test

It is immediately apparent that very few of the partial regression coefficients are statistically significant at conventional levels. The F statistic for the equation as a whole similarly fails to achieve statistical significance even at the 0.25 level. Whereas the simple correlation between the counterfactual residual and affirmative action payments for all 130 female faculty was 0.48, the simple correlation between the counterfactual residual and affirmative action payments made to the 58 actual recipients was only 0.36. These findings suggest that the affirmative action decisionmakers were perhaps more skilled at identifying worthy recipients of affirmative action increments than they were at deciding

how large an increment should be granted. Of course, it can be argued that
identifying worthy receipients is not a very demanding task when 87 of the 130
female faculty have negative counterfactual residuals prior to affirmative action.

Reversing the Factual-Counterfactual Direction

Our empirical work thus far has concentrated upon a factual-counterfactual
methodology. Since we have been interested primarily in the possibility of sex
discrimination in salaries against female faculty, we estimated a counterfactual for
each female faculty member based upon what that female faculty member would
have been paid had she been paid according to the determinants of male faculty
salaries. We then compared that counterfactual salary to the female faculty
member's actual salary, and termed the difference the "counterfactual residual."

In our review of previous empirical studies in Chapter 4, we noted that a
judicial decision in the Eighth Circuit Court of Appeals in the state of Nebraska
had forced the University of Nebraska to extend affirmative action to male
faculty as well as female faculty.[7] That is, the University of Nebraska was
ordered to raise the salaries of a selected group of male faculty to the same
levels to which a selected group of female faculty had been raised.

The analogous process in the context of this study is to raise the salaries
of male faculty at Illinois State University to their counterfactual levels. In this
case, however, the counterfactual estimate of each male faculty member's salary—
which indicates what the male faculty member in question would have been paid
had he been paid according to the same determinants as female faculty—is then
compared to the actual salary of male faculty in order to obtain a counterfactual
residual pertaining to men.

Reversing the direction of the factual-counterfactual analysis is not idle work
where affirmative action is concerned. The Appeals court decision involving the
University of Nebraska (reviewed in Chapter 4) makes it clear that the same criteria or techniques must be applied to all faculty members in an affirmative
action program. While that was not done at Illinois State University, it is of
interest to determine the number of male faculty whose actual salaries were less
than their counterfactual salaries in the 1973-74 academic year when the most
significant affirmative action salary increments were dispensed.

The mean counterfactual salary of the 429 male faculty in the 1973-74 academic year was $1,728 per month. The actual mean salary of these same male
faculty members was $1,743 per month. The difference between these two
salary magnitudes, $15 per month, represents a mean estimate of the extent to

which male faculty were overpaid relative to their counterfactual salaries.[b] The difference, however, is not statistically significant at the 0.10 level.

A closer reading of the University of Nebraska case, however, reveals that the decision of the court required the University of Nebraska to raise the salaries of any male faculty members who were found to be below the counterfactual criterion salary. The raise was to be equal to the difference between the actual salary of the male faculty member and the counterfactual criterion salary (which was not derived in the same fashion as the counterfactual salaries generated in this chapter). It is quite possible for individual male faculty members to have counterfactual salaries greater than their actual salaries, even though this is not true in a mean sense for all male faculty members as a class.

Of the 429 male faculty members at Illinois State University in the academic year 1973-74 who were included in the data set, 260 (61 percent) had counterfactual salaries which were greater than their actual salaries. The mean difference for these 260 male faculty was $143 per month. The annual cost (on a 9-month basis) of raising the actual salaries of these 260 male faculty to their counterfactual levels would have been almost $335,000. By way of contrast, the second year of affirmative action payments made to female faculty involved only about $35,000 in payments on a 9-month basis.

The striking moral to the analysis in this subsection is that the decision of the Appeals court re the University of Nebraska has tremendous financial implications for the operation of affirmative action salary-increment programs everywhere. The cost of operating an affirmative action salary program for male faculty would have been almost 10 times as much as the cost of the program actually carried out for female faculty at Illinois State University. The expense of extending affirmative action procedures to all faculty may be so great that there may exist a strong temptation to have no affirmative action salary programs at all. This is undoubtedly one of the most important empirical findings of this study.

A Semilog Functional Form

Earlier in this chapter, the possibility of a semilog functional form was

---

[b]This finding is not inconsistent with our previous finding that the affirmative action salary increments eliminated mean salary discrimination against female faculty as a class. The previous finding was generated by a factual-counterfactual analysis based upon male faculty salary determinants. The current analysis is based upon female faculty salary determinants. The two approaches need not yield the same results if the two salary structures differ.

suggested and outlined in Equation (5.2). The attractiveness of a semilog form lies primarily in its relation to existing theory. Ben-Porath has demonstrated that the semilog form is a reduced form obtained from a series of appealing structural equations.[8] There seems reason, therefore, to estimate a semilog form utilizing the usual independent variables in the model.

The semilog empirical results which the authors obtained were generally quite similar to those reported in this chapter. Considerably more instability was evidenced with respect to the sign and magnitude of the partial regression coefficient on the *SEX* variable. Several of the changes from year to year were sufficiently volatile to cast doubt upon the validity of the equations estimated. This is an initial reason why the empirical work presented in this chapter does not feature the semilog form.

A secondary reason why the semilog form seems unnecessary in this case relates to the specification of experience-related independent variables. The semilog form of Ben-Porath reflects, among other things, a particular view of the temporal shape of the earnings of individuals, particularly females, over time. Females and individuals with predegree experience are expected to have flatter earnings profiles than males and those individuals with little or no pre-degree experience. The semilog form is one way in which such a possibility can be recognized. Another way in which this possibility can be taken into account is by specifying both linear and quadratic terms for experience-related variables. That has been done in this study where, for example, both *AGE* and *AGESQ* have been specified as independent variables.

Much of the discussion relating to the relevance and specification of experience-related variables, however, turns upon the actual productivity and performance of particular faculty as they grow older and more experienced. The specification of quadratic terms is clearly necessary if one has no reliable measure of the differential productivity and performance of individual faculty members. The quadratic terms of the experience-related variables should pick up any enhancement or decline in the performance of individual faculty as those faculty become older and more experienced. A strong point in favor of the data set underlying this study is that productivity and performance data for individual faculty are available. Hence, the quadratic terms seem less necessary from an a priori standpoint. The same conclusion holds concerning a semilog functional form, which seeks to address itself to presumed nonlinearities in the relationship between salary and experience-related variables.

There is a final argument which can be utilized to justify the "linear-in-parameters" specification of Equation (5.1) rather than the semilog specification of Equation (5.2). Despite the fact that the semilog form is an acceptable re-duced form emanating from structural equations, the linear-in-parameters func-tional form of Equation (5.1), which is the basis for the empirical work reported in this chapter, need not be disgarded. Following Griliches,[9] the counterfactual estimate upon which the empirical work is based can be regarded as a "hedonic counterfactual index" of what an individual faculty member would be paid were he or she paid according to the same salary determinants as those of the opposite sex. Instead of talking about automobile quality changes, as did Griliches, we talk about changes in faculty characteristics and their effects upon the counterfactual salary. We wish to know the determinants of this counterfactual salary. The semilog form is not a necessity in this case.

Interaction Terms

We have already reviewed the argument of Johnson and Stafford[10] that not only is there a relationship between salary and independent variables such as age and sex, but also there may be a simultaneous relationship between the age and sex variables themselves. Johnson and Stafford attempted to allow for this possibility by specifying interaction terms, for example, *FEM* X *XPO*, which is the independent variable designating female status times the independent variable representing the faculty member's years of postdegree experience.

Unfortunately, Johnson and Stafford found that their model was only ". . . weakly improved by specifying these interactions."[11] The inclusion of interaction terms such as *SEX* X *YEARS* in the current study as independent variables was similarly unproductive. Interaction variables do not appear to have statistically significant relationships with faculty salaries when the usual variables in the model are also taken into account.

Multicollinearity

The basic model outlined in Equation (5.1) and utilized thereafter includes over twenty independent variables. Some of the independent variables, for example, *YEARS* and *AGE*, might possibly be correlated with each other and therefore are possible nominees for problem areas relating to multicollinearity. The possibility, detection, and consequences of multicollinearity among independent variables in regression have been discussed frequently. The groundbreaking work by Farrar and Glauber is an example.[12] Multicollinearity problems do not appear to be severe in this study, however.

Appendix B reports a zero-order correlation matrix among the dependent variable and all independent variables utilized in the regular model for the 1973-74 academic year. The simple correlations are generally impressively low and do not present an apparent problem.

Summary of Empirical Findings

Multiple regression, linear in all parameters, was carried out in order to make a judgment about the existence of sex discrimination in faculty salaries at Illinois State University. The empirical evidence does not allow the unqualified conclusion that sex discrimination existed in the faculty salary structure because possible sex differences in labor force participation rates, quit rates, and expected future productivity were not explicitly taken into account. However, the regressions which form the basis of the empirical evidence do contain unprecedented peer merit evaluations of each faculty member's productivity in three areas: teaching, scholarly productivity, and service. The regressions also utilize both linear and quadratic terms for experience-related variables, and therefore indirectly reflect the possible sex differences noted above.

The regressions which form the basis of the empirical evidence are of two types. The first set of regressions specified sex as a dummy variable. The sign of the partial regression coefficient on the sex dummy variable indicates the partial relationship between faculty salaries and sex, holding constant all other independent variables in the model. The second set of regressions was part of a factual-counterfactual methodology in which a determination was made with respect to what female faculty members would have been paid had they been compensated according to the same determinants as male faculty. This necessitated the estimation of a salary equation for male faculty only. The estimated coefficients from this equation were then used to generate a counterfactual estimate of what female faculty would have earned had they been paid according to the determinants of male faculty salaries. The factual-counterfactual methodology corresponds most closely to the requirements of the law relative to making judgments concerning sex discrimination. Factual-counterfactualism allows the entire regression structure to respond to the influence of sex rather than holding all other variables constant.

The difference in dollars between the actual salary of the female faculty member and the counterfactual estimate of her salary was termed the "counterfactual residual" and was used as the basis for making a judgment about the existence of sex discrimination in the salary structure as a whole and against individual faculty as well. The identity and characteristics of those female faculty who received affirmative action salary increments in either the 1972-73 or the 1973-74 academic year were also scrutinized. Finally, the overall and the individual effects of the affirmative action salary program upon sex discrimination were examined.

The major conclusions are:

(1) Disregarding possible sex differences in labor force participation rates, quit rates, and expected future productivity, sex discrimination in salaries against female faculty did exist at Illinois State University prior to the implementation of an affirmative action salary program.

(2) The two years of affirmative action salary payments (the 1972-73 and 1973-74 academic years) eliminated mean sex discrimination against female faculty as a class, although the amount of that sex discrimination was statistically

insignificant at the 0.10 level prior to the beginning of the second year of affirmative action salary payments.

(3) Elimination of mean sex discrimination against female faculty as a class did not eliminate sex discrimination against many individual female faculty, nor did it reduce any existing sex discrimination in favor of female faculty. After the second year of affirmative action salary payments, 66 of the 130 female faculty in the data set still had actual salaries which were less than their counterfactual salaries. This was true despite the fact that the mean counterfactual salary of female faculty as a class was found to be $7 less per month than the actual salary of the same female faculty.

(4) Statistically significant sex discrimination against female faculty did not reappear in the 1974-75 or 1975-76 academic years. The empirical results did reveal, however, statistically significant salary discrimination in favor of minority (nonwhite, non-Caucasian) faculty in the 1975-76 academic year.

(5) The 66 female faculty who were recipients of affirmative action salary increments in the 1972-73 academic year, and the 53 female faculty who received affirmative action salary payments in the 1973-74 academic year, were generally (relative to male faculty): (a) of lower academic rank; (b) recipients of slightly lower peer merit evaluations of their teaching performance; (c) recipients of noticeably lower peer merit evaluations of their scholarly productivity; (d) disproportionately found in low market demand disciplines and specialties; (e) 5 years older in mean age; (f) in possession of the doctorate 2.63 years less; and (g) underpaid by a mean of $87 per month.

(6) The simple correlation between the size of the affirmative action payment (positive or zero) given female faculty and the counterfactual residual of those same female faculty was 0.48 in the 1973-74 academic year. This indicates that the identification of deserving recipients of affirmative action salary payments (in view of the law) was broadly correct.

(7) The simple correlation between the size of the affirmative action payment (positive payments only) and the counterfactual residual of those same female faculty fell to 0.36. This may mean that the affirmative action decision-makers were more skilled at identifying female faculty who were deserving than they were at determining how large an affirmative action salary payment should be made to those deserving faculty. This conclusion is given indirect support by the fact that the conventional independent variables in the model were largely unable to explain the size of affirmative action salary payments actually made to female faculty.

(8) The decision of the court in *Regents* v. *Dawes* ordered the University of Nebraska to raise the salaries of all male faculty in the same fashion that the university had previously raised the salaries of female faculty via an affirmative action salary program. The same process, if applied to the 430 male faculty in the data set at Illinois State University in the academic year 1973-74, would have required about $335,000, which was almost 10 times as much money as

was actually expended on affirmative action increments to females in that academic year.

(9) The use of a semilog functional form and the specification of interaction terms did little to enhance the empirical results.

(10) Despite the large number of variables involved in the study, multicollinearity problems appear to have been minimal.

6 Implications and Conclusions

Facts are enemies of The Truth.

Perhaps the greatest difficulty which must be overcome when one reports an empirical study in the area of sex discrimination and affirmative action is the pre-conceptions of the listening or reading audience. Like Don Quixote, numerous individuals, even those academics who pride themselves upon their objectivity and dispassionate attitudes, have preconceived notions about what the results of any such empirical study should be. Academic precincts do not lack for those individuals who are ardent feminists and see discrimination in every corner. Neither is there a shortage of individuals who instinctively regard all claims of discrimination as baseless and all affirmative action programs as an unwarranted waste of time and resources. There is little that has been said in this study that will alter such dogmatic viewpoints. This study is addressed to those individuals who have not beforehand decided what "The Truth" is.

The factual-counterfactual methodology which is the center of the empirical analysis presented in Chapter 5 closely reflects the requirements of the law in the area of affirmative action. The law requires that the same evaluative standards and the same reward structures be applied to both women and men. The standard and structures that are applied may be regarded by some as being evidence of outright stupidity. Nonetheless, as long as the standards and structures do not distinguish between the sexes, and are applied evenhandedly to both sexes, they are permissible. There is nothing in current law or regulations which, for example, states that a merit system of determining salary increments is preferred, or is not preferred, to a salary schedule which is based upon longevity factors. It is true, however, that affirmative action regulations seem often to equate longevity with meritorious performance.

Using the factual-counterfactual model, we have found that mean sex discrimination in faculty salaries did exist at Illinois State University prior to the initiation of an affirmative action salary program. Note, however, that the validity of this study does not depend upon whether or not sex discrimination did or did not exist at Illinois State University. The point is that an affirmative action salary program was undertaken, and it is this which we examine.

A. Cervantes, *Don Quijote de la Mancha,* as quoted in Angel Rosenblatt, *La Lengua del Quijote* (Madrid: Editorial Gredos, S.A., 1971), p. 250.

121

The salary increments dispensed as a part of the affirmative action salary program eliminated this discrimination against female faculty as a class. This finding, however, hides a great deal. First, numerous individual female faculty members remained underpaid relative to their counterfactual salary after the affirmative action salary program had been terminated. Second, the magnitude of the affirmative action salary increments given to certain female faculty seems to have been somewhat arbitrary in nature.

It is possible for one to dismiss our finding of sex discrimination in salaries by arguing that sex differences in labor force participation rates, quit rates, and expected future productivity have not been held constant. This is a valid point, and there is, in view of the empirical evidence available on these issues, reason to believe that our estimates of the amount of sex discrimination in salaries are upper-bound estimates. It was not possible in this study to control for labor force participation and the like with the cross-sectional data available. Nonetheless, the implications of economic theory (particularly that dealing with the specificity of human capital) and available empirical evidence make further research into this area an extremely high-priority item. We desperately need time-series observations of the labor force behavior and productivity of male and female faculty.

The law does not permit utilizing sex as a proxy for other variables. For example, even if sex differences in labor force participation rates exist, it is not legally permissible to penalize female faculty as a class because of that fact. Differences in labor force participation rates, quit rates, or expected future productivity are a legally permissible reason for the existence of salary differentials only when those differences in labor force participation, and the like, are applied on an individual basis. Hence, if Mary Smith has a lower labor force participation rate, a higher quit rate, and lower expected future productivity than John Smith, it is legally permissible to pay John Smith more than Mary Smith if all other characteristics of the Smiths are identical. On the other hand, the law prohibits paying Mary Smith less than John Smith merely because Mary Smith is a female and empirical evidence points to lower labor force participation rates on the part of females.[a]

This study has, in a cross-sectional context, proceeded further than any other study in terms of including most of the relevant variables in a salary-determination equation. Indeed, it is possible to argue that the inclusion of current-year peer merit evaluations and the specification of quadratic terms in the experience-related variables may even pick up sex differences in labor force participation rates, quit rates, and expected future productivity. Further, the fact that this study has estimated separate salary equations for males and females also allows for potential sex differences in these variables to be reflected in the

---

[a]Class distinctions, per se, are not illegal. For example, it is legally permissible to automatically compensate full professors more than instructors as long as sex has nothing to do with entrance to those ranks.

estimated coefficients. Once again, however, we need additional empirical evidence in this area before we can reach more definitive conclusions about the relevancy or irrelevancy of labor force participation and similar factors.

The transferability of the empirical evidence produced in this study to other colleges and universities must be considered. Illinois State University is a state-supported university with about 20,000 students. Although it offers doctoral-level degree programs, it is classified as a II-A school by the American Association of University Professors. A large number of similar universities exist in nearly every state. More importantly, the problems and promise of affirmative action are common to nearly every school in academia. Hence, while the authors cannot state firmly that the empirical evidence of Chapter 5 is relevant to other situations, they have strong reason to believe so.

Resource Allocation, Equity, and Efficiency

We have seen that the affirmative action salary increments went primarily to those female faculty who were relatively less productive, more elderly, less qualified in terms of degree status, and more likely to hold an appointment in an excess-supply discipline. It does not immediately strike one that the provision of extra compensation for such faculty is the recipe for building an excellent university. A high-level university administrator who must allocate scarce financial resources might well think seriously about the opportunity cost of such an activity. Each dollar used to compensate such faculty, who are apparently less mobile and who apparently have lower wage elasticities of supply, cannot be used to compensate other faculty, purchase computer time, or add books to the library. Further, it is not clear that additional salary rewards to such faculty will stimulate additional or improved performance.

The Becker variety of discrimination model invokes perfect competition. In such a world, an academic administrator will increase productivity and increase both private and social economic efficiency by dispensing affirmative action salary increments. If one views the university as a monopsonist, however, then the reverse is true. Affirmative action salary increments may be equitable and just, but they are probably not economically efficient either in a private context or a social context. Economic efficiency dictates that the wage-discriminating monopsonist should pay lower wages (*ceteris paribus*) to female faculty *if* female faculty have lower wage elasticities of supply. This action will make available additional funds for other academic purposes.

As we have seen, there is strong reason to believe that the mean wage elasticity of supply of female faculty is actually less than the corresponding figure for male faculty. This means that affirmative action payments, even when justified by a factual-counterfactual model such as that developed in this study, may well be equitable, just, and eminently desirable in the eyes of most reasonable individuals, but they are probably not economically efficient. The law (particularly the Equal Pay Act of 1963), the regulations of agencies such as the EEOC, and the implications of the factual-counterfactual model must be viewed as equity rather than efficiency instruments. Affirmative action salary programs are primarily equity programs. They are probably not economically efficient, particularly when a short-run viewpoint is taken.

It should be noted parenthetically that it is possible to construct a long-run efficiency argument for affirmative action. In this view, continued exercise of wage-discriminating monopsonist behavior will discourage females from entering the labor force and will lower the productivity of those females already in the labor force. In the long run, then, it is not economically efficient for either the firm or the society to engage in discriminatory behavior. The validity of this argument depends upon (among other things) the present value of the efficiency gains obtained from short-run discrimination vis-à-vis the efficiency losses that might obtain in the long run if discrimination occurs.

A major problem associated with the argument of long-run gains relates to the size of the long-run gains that will be realized. In Chapter 3 we noted that the productivity gains from the elimination of occupational overcrowding by race were minimal.[1] While we have no direct evidence upon the size of productivity gains from the elimination of overcrowding and salary discrimination against females, the evidence relating to race discrimination does not inspire confidence in large estimates.

There is additionally the matter of the amount of economic resources of all kinds (personnel, paper, time, and so forth) that is devoted to the administration and enforcement of affirmative action laws and regulations. These resources are of such magnitude that colleges and universities are petitioning the federal government for assistance and financial aid in coping with this new demand. The antagonism of some to affirmative action programs seems sometimes to stem more from the cost of satisfying affirmative action laws and regulations than from an inherent objection to the equity considerations involved. In this context, the imposition of new affirmative action requirements is viewed by some as an undesirable part of a myriad of new federal regulations and controls that seem to apply to academia. As Kingman Brewster, the president of Yale University, has put it, "The temptation is overwhelming to see to it that the recipient of the federal dollar is virtuous in all respects."[2]

In any case, the cost of complying with affirmative action requirements is not trivial. The *economic* cost of operating an affirmative action salary program at Illinois State University was undoubtedly greater than the $35,000 actually distributed to 53 female faculty members in the 1973-74 academic year. For example, the annual salary of the affirmative action officer for women was by itself about two-thirds of the $35,000 total.[b] When the value of the human

---

[b]It should be pointed out that the affirmative action officer for women at Illinois State University usually teaches one or more classes during a typical semester, so that the

time and computer resources connected with identifying affirmative action salary recipients is taken into account, there is little doubt that the administrative costs associated with achieving equity were higher than the total amount of salary payments made in that regard.

It is not clear, of course, that the fact that the administrative costs of achieving equity were greater than the salary costs of doing so has any immediate relevance for policy making. Equity and economic efficiency are not necessarily the same thing; their paths frequently part in the minds of many individuals. What the results of this study do indicate is that the cost of achieving a proclaimed equity goal can be quite high in terms of visible resources expended as well as in terms of less visible efficiency losses. This cost must be weighed against the results that could be achieved from alternative uses of the resources. For example, if the economic cost of a particular affirmative action salary program is (in a *given* year) $100,000, then one must ask whether this is better or worse than having an additional six to eight assistant-professor slots in the university in question.

Some readers may object to the authors having "placed a price upon equity and justice." Yet, equity and justice do have a price just as there is also a price associated with the avoidance of disease, the prevention of automobile accidents, and the educating of additional students. It is most assuredly not the task of the authors to decide either for the reader or for society whether affirmative action programs "are worth it." What this study seeks to do is identify the economic costs, benefits, and effects of the operation of affirmative action programs. Each citizen may then mull over this information and reach a decision concerning the viability and need for affirmative action programs. The authors have already stated their normative views in the first chapter. Those views, however, should not obscure the economic choices which actually are implied by the operation of affirmative action programs.

Regents v. *Dawes:* The Iceberg of Affirmative Action

Our review of existing empirical evidence concerning the operation and effects of affirmative action programs in Chapter 4 discussed the landmark status of the decision of the court in *Regents* v. *Dawes.*[3] The implications of this decision for the operation and cost of affirmative action salary programs are immense. In *Regents* v. *Dawes,* the U.S. Court of Appeals, Eighth Circuit, stated that any

---

entirety of her salary should not be attributed solely to affirmative action. Similarly, the affirmative action officer is and has been involved in numerous activities other than the affirmative action salary-increment program. It is, therefore, not clear what proportion of salary of the affirmative action officer should be attributed to running the affirmative action salary-increment program during the 1973-74 academic year.

salary-equalization procedure utilized by a university or firm must apply equally
to both sexes. The court found the University of Nebraska in violation of the
Equal Pay Act of 1963 for increasing the salaries of a selected group of female
faculty to a counterfactually determined level without doing the same for male
faculty in similar circumstances. The *Regents* v. *Dawes* decision appears to require that affirmative action programs apply to both sexes and to ethnic groups.

The idea that affirmative action programs must attempt to eliminate salary
sex discrimination against both female and male faculty is relatively noncontro-
versial in nature. Discrimination is discrimination, whoever the unfortunate
target. The relevant point is that the cost of eliminating identifiable salary
deficiencies for male faculty, whether or not the deficiencies stem from discrimination, can be great. In the case at hand, the cost of bringing the salaries of all
male faculty up to their counterfactual level would have been almost 10 times the
actual monies actually expended upon affirmative action payments to female
faculty in the 1973-74 academic year. The administrator who is aware of the
import of *Regents* v. *Dawes,* and the cost of including male faculty in affirmative action salary programs, may be somewhat cautious about initiating such a
compensatory program in the first place.

The empirical evidence presented in Chapter 5 indicated that, prior to
affirmative action, the percent of female faculty who were underpaid relative
to their counterfactual salary was much greater than the percent of male faculty
who were in a similar circumstance. Nonetheless, the numerical predominance
of males in the Illinois State University faculty would have caused the cost of
including male faculty in the affirmative action salary program to increase almost
10 times. When a large proportion of female faculty are underpaid, female faculty
are likely to demand the implementation of an affirmative action salary program.
The administration that does not also include male faculty in that program stands
in apparent violation of *Regents* v. *Dawes* and would seem to be inviting a legal
suit by affected male faculty. Therein lies the quandry for the administrator.
It remains to be seen whether this quandry leads to a decrease in the number and
size of affirmative action salary programs.

Efficiency and/or Equity: Once Again

Real or imagined conflicts between that which is efficient and that which is
equitable are as old as the human race. The most efficient means to accomplish
a given end is not always the way in which people wish to achieve that end. Indeed, those who argue for efficiency rather than equity are often regarded as
Philistines.

Efficiency implies achieving a given end at the least possible cost, or, what
is the other side of the same coin, maximizing output or results given a certain
expenditure of resources. Economic efficiency does not always appeal to

individuals as being equitable or just. For example, economic efficiency is obtained when each worker receives a wage equal to the value of his or her marginal product. One can easily visualize cases involving mentally retarded or physically incapacitated individuals where the value of the marginal product of such individuals is negligible or even zero. Hence, economic efficiency dictates that a similarly negligible or zero wage should be paid such individuals. Most societies have rebelled against the application of efficiency principles in this fashion. Altruistic and humane considerations lead to the compensation of such individuals despite their lack of productivity.

The trade-off between efficiency and equity is often very real. Some efficiency must usually be scrapped when the order of the day is equity, and less equitable situations seem often to rear their heads when efficiency is the byword. The discussion of the nature of this trade-off and how and where it should be made is a hardy perennial. A recent example is Arthur Okun's *Equality and Efficiency*.[4]

The tools of economic analysis are not particularly suited to the solution or moral-ethical dilemmas. Hence, it is not possible to state that the apparent lack of economic efficiency which we observe in affirmative action programs is unethical, immoral, or inequitable. What we can say is that such economic inefficiency forces society to sacrifice certain other goals that it might have achieved.

Most individuals (including the authors) regard sex discrimination as undesirable. Many individuals believe that the maxim of "equal pay for equal work" is the essence of justice in the labor markets which characterize universities. Neither of these value judgments, however, is necessarily consistent with economic efficiency in the imperfectly competitive world in which we live.

Our empirical evidence leads to the conclusion that affirmative action programs must be considered to be the instruments of equity rather than the instruments of economic efficiency. A wide range of viewpoints exists with respect to how society should strike the appropriate balance between efficiency and equity when the two conflict. An intelligent decision, however, requires accurate knowledge about the nature of the conflict or trade-off involved. The function of this book, hopefully achieved, has been to increase our knowledge of the economic choices that confront us when affirmative action programs are contemplated. Given the lack of reliable empirical evidence available, this tome is truly a small candle lighting a vast darkness. It is the hope of the authors that this book will not only stimulate discussion of the economics of affirmative action, but also will serve as the first of many other studies in the same arena.

Appendix A: Law and Documents Relevant to Sex Discrimination

The Equal Pay Act of 1963

Declaration of Purpose

Sec. 3. Section 6 of the Fair Labor Standards Act of 1938, as amended (29 U.S.C.A. et seq.), is amended by adding thereto a new subsection (d) as follows:

(d) (1) No employer having employees subject to any provisions of this section shall discriminate, within any establishment in which such employees are employed, between employees on the basis of sex by paying wages to employees in such establishment at a rate less than the rate at which he pays wages to employees of the opposite sex in such establishment for equal work on jobs the performance of which requires equal skill, effort, and responsibility, and which are performed under similar working conditions, except where such payment is made pursuant to (i) a seniority system; (ii) a merit system; (iii) a system which measures earnings by quantity or quality of production; or (iv) a differential based on any other factor other than sex: *Provided*, That an employer who is paying a wage rate differential in violation of this subsection shall not, in order to comply with the provisions of this subsection, reduce the wage rate of any employee.

Title VII of the Civil Rights Act of 1964, as amended by the Equal Employment Opportunity Act of 1972—Equal Employment Opportunity

Discrimination because of Race, Color, Religion, Sex, or National Origin

Sec. 703. (a) It shall be an unlawful employment practice for an employer
(1) to fail or refuse to hire or to discharge any individual, or otherwise to discriminate against any individual with respect to his compensation, terms, conditions, or privileges of employment, because of such individual's race, color,

129

religion, sex, or national origin; or (2) to limit, segregate, or classify his employees or applicants for employment in any way which would deprive or tend to deprive any individual of employment opportunities or otherwise adversely affect his status as an employee, because of such individual's race, color, religion, sex, or national origin. (As amended March 24, 1972, P.L. 92-261, Sec. 8.)

(b) It shall be unlawful employment practice for any employment agency to fail or refuse to refer for employment, or otherwise to discriminate against, any individual because of his race, color, religion, sex, or national origin, or to classify or refer for employment any individual on the basis of his race, color, religion, sex, or national origin.

Title VII of the Civil Rights Act of 1964, as amended by the Equal Employment Opportunity Act of 1972—Equal Employment Opportunity

Equal Employment Opportunity Commission

Sec. 705. (a) There is hereby created a Commission to be known as the Equal Employment Opportunity Commission, which shall be composed of five members, not more than three of whom shall be members of the same political party.

Prevention of Unlawful Employment Practices (EEOC Authority)

Sec. 706. (a) The Commission is empowered, as hereinafter provided, to prevent any person from engaging in any unlawful employment practice as set forth in section 703 or 704 of this title. (As amended March 24, 1972, P.L. 92-261, Sec. 4.)

(b) Whenever a charge is filed by or on behalf of a person claiming to be aggrieved, or by a member of the Commission, alleging that an employer, employment agency, labor organization, or joint labor organization, or joint labor-management committee controlling apprenticeship or other training or retraining, including on-the-job training programs, has engaged in an unlawful employment practice, the Commission shall serve a notice of the charge (including the date, place and circumstances of the alleged unlawful employment practice) on such employer, employment agency, labor organization, or joint labor-management committee (hereinafter referred to as the "respondent") within ten days, and shall make an investigation thereof. Charges shall be in writing under oath or affirmation and shall contain such information and be in such form as the Commission requires. Charges shall not be made public by the Commission. If the Commission determines after such investigation that there is not reasonable cause to believe that the charge is true, it shall dismiss the charge and promptly notify the person claiming to be aggrieved and the respondent of its action. In determining whether reasonable cause exists, the Commission shall accord substantial weight to final findings and orders made by State or local authorities in proceedings commenced under State or local law pursuant to the requirements of subsections (c) and (d). If the Commission determines after such investigation that there is reasonable cause to believe that the charge is true, the Commission shall endeavor to eliminate any such alleged unlawful employment practice by informal methods of conference, conciliation, and persuasion. Nothing said or done during and as a part of such informal endeavors may be made public by the Commission, its officers or employees, or used as evidence in a subsequent proceeding without the written consent of the persons concerned. Any person who makes public information in violation of this subsection shall be fined not more than $1,000 or imprisoned for not more than one year, or both. The Commission shall make its determination on reasonable cause as promptly as possible and, so far as practicable, not later than one hundred and twenty days from the filing of the charge or, where applicable under subsection (c) or (d), from the date upon which the Commission is authorized to take action with respect to the charge. (As amended March 24, 1972, P.L. 92-261, Sec. 4.)

Revised Order No. 4, Affirmative Action Programs 41 C.F.R. 60-2

(1) In determining whether minorities are being underutilized in any job classification the contractor will consider at least all of the following factors:

(i) The minority population of the labor area surrounding the facility;

(ii) The size of the minority unemployment force in the labor area surrounding the facility;

(iii) The percentage of the minority work force as compared with the total work force in the immediate labor area;

(iv) The general availability of minorities having requisite skills in the immediate labor area;

(v) The availability of minorities having requisite skills in an area in which the contractor can reasonably recruit;

(vi) The availability of promotable and transferable minorities within the contractor's organization;

(vii) The existence of training institutions capable of training persons in the requisite skills; and

(viii) The degree of training which the contractor is reasonably able to undertake as a means of making all job classes available to women.

Title IX Interpretation from the U.S. Department of Health, Education and Welfare Fact Sheet, June 18, 1974, p. 2.

The proposed regulation forbids discrimination by sex in most educational institutions—colleges, universities, secondary and elementary schools and pre-schools—which receive Federal funds.

It would cover three major areas: admission, treatment of students, and employment. With respect to admission to educational institutions, the proposed regulation is designed to ensure students equal access—with certain exceptions specified by Congress. With respect to treatment to students and employment, the proposal provides for nondiscrimination and equality of opportunity.

The proposed regulation would affect, among others, virtually all public school systems in the country, as well as almost 2,500 institutions of post-secondary education, currently receiving Federal funds.

By Congressional exemption, the proposed regulation would not apply at all to military schools; nor would it apply to religious schools if that would be inconsistent with the controlling religious tenets of these schools. In addition, Congress exempted, from the admissions requirements only, private undergraduate colleges, non-vocational elementary and secondary schools, and certain public undergraduate schools which have traditionally and continually been single-sex.

The proposed regulation also would prohibit discrimination in employment, on the basis of sex, by educational institutions.

Appendix B: Zero-order Correlation Matrix, 1973-74

Table B-1

	INST	ASST	ASSO	FULL	PHD	YEARS
ASST	-0.187					
ASSO	-0.126	-0.551				
FULL	-0.115	-0.504	-0.341			
PHD	-0.286	-0.460	0.289	0.368		
YEARS	-0.172	-0.552	0.092	0.629	0.602	
TENURE	-0.292	-0.288	0.147	0.319	0.028	0.320
TEA1	-0.015	0.081	-0.044	-0.041	-0.101	-0.061
TEA2	0.053	0.015	0.015	-0.059	-0.042	0.098
TEA3	0.028	0.093	-0.073	-0.045	-0.020	-0.005
TEA4	-0.071	-0.128	0.073	0.106	0.071	-0.064
SCH1	0.113	0.064	-0.034	-0.092	-0.170	-0.070
SCH2	0.065	0.152	-0.100	-0.104	-0.158	0.017
SCH3	-0.079	-0.043	-0.011	0.100	0.115	0.049
SCH4	-0.044	-0.166	0.150	0.058	0.138	-0.037
SERV1	-0.027	0.040	0.008	-0.043	-0.016	0.072
SERV2	0.055	0.200	-0.072	-0.185	-0.156	-0.133
SERV3	-0.026	-0.011	0.004	0.021	0.039	0.067
SERV4	-0.019	-0.205	0.067	0.178	0.117	0.044
AFF	0.025	0.104	-0.099	-0.029	-0.154	-0.093
SEX	-0.184	-0.116	0.136	0.078	0.243	0.149
RACE	-0.044	0.013	-0.088	0.097	0.051	0.020
YRB	0.161	0.240	0.004	-0.361	0.023	-0.450
YRR	-0.011	-0.135	0.204	-0.049	0.178	-0.237
MKTLOW	0.014	0.007	-0.011	-0.003	-0.123	-0.079
MKTMED	0.006	-0.011	0.008	0.000	0.104	0.081
MKTHI	-0.047	0.007	0.007	0.006	0.045	-0.002
AGE	-0.161	-0.240	-0.004	0.361	-0.023	0.450
YRSR	0.011	0.135	-0.204	0.049	-0.178	0.237
AGESQ	-0.154	-0.222	-0.018	0.351	-0.027	0.458
YRSRSQ	-0.029	0.093	-0.155	0.067	-0.157	0.219
YEARSQ	-0.101	-0.384	-0.019	0.516	0.356	0.919

Table B-2

	TENURE	TEA1	TEA2	TEA3	TEA4	SCH1
TEA1	0.045					
TEA2	−0.017	−0.036				
TEA3	0.007	−0.067	−0.456			
TEA4	0.006	−0.052	−0.357	−0.652		
SCH1	0.055	0.203	0.225	−0.067	−0.150	
SCH2	−0.004	−0.005	0.201	0.077	−0.248	−0.178
SCH3	0.056	−0.054	−0.159	0.038	0.105	−0.174
SCH4	−0.083	−0.039	−0.168	−0.094	0.250	−0.124
SERV1	0.053	0.359	0.067	−0.014	−0.096	0.211
SERV2	−0.158	0.003	0.329	−0.000	−0.276	0.156
SERV3	0.057	−0.055	−0.147	0.203	−0.078	−0.110
SERV4	0.090	−0.048	−0.194	−0.204	0.390	−0.102
AFF	0.019	−0.020	0.024	−0.016	0.000	0.061
SEX	−0.021	−0.017	−0.031	0.026	−0.000	−0.119
RACE	0.045	0.015	−0.048	−0.001	0.039	−0.030
YRB	−0.538	−0.084	−0.105	0.031	0.063	−0.175
YRR	−0.274	−0.191	−0.186	−0.021	0.206	−0.220
MKTLOW	0.052	0.020	0.015	−0.097	0.090	0.010
MKTMED	−0.027	−0.012	−0.027	0.103	−0.087	0.013
MKTHI	−0.058	−0.016	0.028	−0.011	−0.008	−0.053
AGE	0.538	0.084	0.105	−0.031	−0.063	0.175
YRSR	0.274	0.191	0.186	0.021	−0.206	0.220
AGESQ	0.505	0.100	0.113	−0.033	−0.071	0.184
YRSRSQ	0.257	0.253	0.169	−0.052	−0.125	0.190
YEARSQ	0.260	−0.036	0.145	−0.011	−0.103	−0.029

Table B-3

	SCH2	SCH3	SCH4	SERV1	SERV2	SERV3
SCH3	-0.570					
SCH4	-0.405	-0.396				
SERV1	0.036	-0.072	-0.071			
SERV2	0.143	-0.082	-0.151	-0.090		
SERV3	0.044	0.007	0.001	-0.102	-0.509	
SERV4	-0.198	0.098	0.174	-0.089	-0.444	-0.501
AFF	0.085	-0.078	-0.040	0.003	-0.011	0.026
SEX	-0.044	-0.004	0.118	0.010	0.040	-0.066
RACE	-0.002	0.029	-0.015	0.028	-0.105	-0.004
YRB	-0.093	-0.003	0.199	-0.103	0.060	-0.031
YRR	-0.237	0.116	0.256	-0.130	-0.057	-0.031
MKTLOW	-0.045	0.068	-0.027	-0.007	0.037	-0.044
MKTMED	0.033	-0.068	0.028	0.021	-0.055	0.069
MKTHI	0.028	-0.000	-0.003	-0.030	0.040	-0.054
AGE	0.093	0.003	-0.199	0.103	-0.060	0.031
YRSR	0.237	-0.116	-0.256	0.130	0.057	0.031
AGESQ	0.098	-0.002	-0.204	0.119	-0.055	0.033
YRSRSQ	0.184	-0.092	-0.207	0.145	0.029	0.018
YEARSQ	0.099	-0.000	-0.097	0.108	-0.068	0.060

Table B-4

	SERV4	AFF	SEX	RACE
AFF	-0.016			
SEX	0.023	-0.484		
RACE	0.101	-0.053	0.029	
YRB	-0.003	-0.115	0.161	0.017
YRR	0.125	0.052	0.066	-0.005
MKTLOW	0.015	0.098	-0.103	-0.093
MKTMED	-0.027	-0.073	0.057	0.073
MKTHI	0.026	-0.059	0.107	0.048
AGE	0.003	0.115	-0.161	-0.017
YRSR	-0.125	-0.052	-0.066	0.005
AGESQ	-0.008	0.121	-0.167	-0.012
YRSRSQ	-0.089	-0.037	-0.065	0.016
YEARSQ	-0.023	-0.047	0.078	-0.004

Table B-5

	YRB	YRR	MKTMED	MKTHI
YRR	0.504			
MKTLOW	−0.108	0.002		
MKTMED	0.056	−0.047		
MKTHI	0.120	0.100	−0.195	
AGE	−1.000	−0.504	−0.056	−0.120
YRSR	−0.504	−1.000	0.047	−0.100
AGESQ	−0.994	−0.523	−0.049	−0.113
YRSRSQ	−0.502	−0.927	−0.001	−0.086
YEARSQ	−0.497	−0.320	0.044	−0.018

Table B-6

	AGE	YRSR
AGE		
YRSR	0.504	
AGESQ	0.994	0.523
YRSRSQ	0.502	0.927
YEARSQ	0.497	0.320

Table B-7

	AGESQ	YRSRSQ
YRSRSQ	0.528	
YEARSQ	0.521	0.319

Notes

Chapter 1
Introduction

1. See, for example, *Economic Problems of Women*, Parts 1, 2, and 3, Joint Economic Committee, 93d Congress, 1st Session (Washington, D.C.: Government Printing Office, 1974). See also Robert Tsuchigane and Norton Dodge, *Economic Discrimination against Women in the United States* (Lexington, Mass.: Lexington Books, 1974).
2. An early theoretical source is Gary Becker, *The Economics of Discrimination* (Chicago: University of Chicago Press, 1957). Footnote 1 contains voluminous material concerning the effects of sex discrimination upon productivity.
3. Richard A. Lester, *Antibias Regulations of Universities: Faculty Problems and Their Solutions* (New York: McGraw-Hill Book Company, 1974).
4. See, for example, the views of Mary M. Lepper, Director of Higher Education Division, Office of Civil Rights, Department of Health, Education, and Welfare, as reported in "Affirmative Action Scored," *The Chronicle of Higher Education*, 8 (July 8, 1974), p. 8.
5. "29 Institutions Warned by HEW that U.S. May Withhold Contracts," *Chronicle of Higher Education*, June 23, 1975, p. 1.
6. This action, and a biting critique of it, may be found in Sheila K. Johnson, "It Is Action, but Is It Affirmative?" *The New York Times* Magazine (May 11, 1975), pp. 18-33.
7. "AT&T Agrees to Pay $2.5 Million to Correct EEO Settlement Deficiencies," *Women Today*, 5 (May 26, 1975), p. 64.
8. Ibid.
9. Among the more rigorous salary studies which have dealt directly with the issue of sex discrimination are James V. Koch and John F. Chizmar, "The Influence of Teaching and Other Factors upon Absolute Salaries and Salary Increments at Illinois State University," *Journal of Economic Education*, 5 (Fall 1973), pp. 27-34; Barbara B. Reagan and Betty J. Maynard, "Sex Discrimination in Universities: An Approach through Internal Labor Market Analysis," *Bulletin of the American Association of University Professors*, 64 (June 1974), pp. 419-427; George E. Johnson and Frank P. Stafford, "The Earnings and Promotion of Women Faculty," *American Economic Review*, 64 (December 1974), pp. 888-903; James V. Koch and

137

John F. Chizmar, "Sex Discrimination and Affirmative Action in Faculty Salaries," *Economic Inquiry* (forthcoming). There are many other studies which purport to deal with sex discrimination; however, the great majority of these other studies contain serious methodological flaws and do not actually deal with what an economist terms discrimination.

10. The distinction between positive and normative economics was first made by John Neville Keynes, *The Scope and Method of Political Economy* (London: MacMillan and Company, 1891). It is largely due to Milton Friedman, however, that this distinction has become so popular among modern economists. See Friedman's "The Methodology of Positive Economics," in *Essays in Positive Economics* (Chicago: University of Chicago Press, 1953), pp. 3-43.

Chapter 2
The Legal Setting

1. Martin Gruberg, *Women in American Politics* (Oshkosh, Wis.: Academic Press, 1968), p. 4.

2. Abigail Adams, the wife of John Adams, prevailed upon him, in a series of letters written during the Constitutional Convention, to specifically include women in the broad statements of equality being formulated. John Adams set aside her requests on the ground that they were politically impossible. See Irving Stone, *Those Who Love: A Biographical Novel of Abigail and John Adams* (Garden City: Doubleday, 1965).

3. Alexis de Tocqueville, *Democracy in America*, Part 2, Reeves Translation (1840), in *World's Classics Series* (New York: Galaxy Books, 1947), p. 400.

4. Editorial from the *New York Herald*, 1852, as quoted in Aileen S. Kraditor (ed.), *Up from the Pedestal: Selected Writings in the History of American Feminism* (Chicago: Quadrangle Books, 1968), p. 190.

5. *Reed v. Reed*, 404 U.S. 71, 92S.Ct. 251, 30 L.Ed.2d 225 (1971).

6. The Fourteenth Amendment to the Constitution, reprinted in Paul A. Freund, Arthur E. Sutherland, Mark D. Howe, and Ernest J. Brown, *Constitutional Law: Cases and Other Problems*, Vol. 1 (Boston: Little, Brown and Company, 1961), p. lxxv.

7. Ibid.

8. The Equal Pay Act of 1963 is actually an amendment to the Fair Labor Standards Act of 1938. The quotation above is taken from Section 3, paragraph (d), point (1) of the Equal Pay Act. Relevant portions of the Equal Pay Act are reprinted in Appendix A. The entirety of the Equal Pay Act may be found in *Affirmative Action and Equal Employment: A Guidebook for Employers*, Vol. 1 (Washington, D.C.: Government Printing Office, 1974).

9. See Thomas E. Murphy, "Female Wage Discrimination: A Study of the Equal Pay Act, 1963-1970," *University of Cincinnati Law Review*, 39 (Fall 1970), pp. 615-649.

10. *Shultz v. Wheaton Glass Company*, 421 F.2d 259, cert. denied 398 U.S. 905, 90 S.Ct. 1696, 26 L.Ed.2d 64 (1970).

11. See discussion in Kenneth M. Davidson, Ruth B. Ginsburg, and Herma H. Kay, *Sex-based Discrimination: Text, Cases, and Materials* (St. Paul: West Publishing Company, 1974), pp. 569-573.

12. The precise language of Title VII (Public Law 92-261) may be found in *Affirmative Action and Equal Employment: A Guidebook for Employers* Vol. 1 (Washington, D.C.: GPO, 1974). Relevant portions of Title VII are reprinted in Appendix A.

13. In October 1975, however, the Department of Health, Education, and Welfare scheduled formal hearings concerning a sex discrimination case at the University of Texas. The hearings represent the first formal step in the long process involved in terminating a university's federal contracts. The University of Texas case, which is discussed under the heading of Executive Order 11,246, constitutes the first time that sex discrimination proceedings have ever been carried this far. At stake are approximately $20 million worth of federal contracts held by the University of Texas. See "Sex-Bias Hearings: Move to Halt U.S. Funds for University of Texas," *Chronicle of Higher Education* (October 14, 1975), p. 12.

14. Section 703, paragraph (e), of Title VII. See *Affirmative Action and Equal Employment: A Guidebook for Employers.*

15. *Phillips v. Martin Marietta Corporation* 400 U.S. 542, 90 S.Ct. 496, 27 L.Ed. 2d 613 (1971).

16. *Sprogis v. United Airlines*, Inc. 444 F.2d 1194, cert. denied 404 U.S. 991, 92 S.Ct. 536, 30 L.Ed.2d 543 (1971).

17. This principle has been affirmed in *Diaz v. Pan-American Airways*, 442 F.2d 385 (5th Cir., 1971); *Rosenfeld v. Southern Pacific Company*, 444 F.2d 1219 (9th Cir., 1971); and, *Griggs v. Duke Power Company*, 401 U.S. 424 (1971).

18. "Government's First Complaint: University of Maryland Charged with Bias," *Chronicle of Higher Education* (October 28, 1975), p. 10.

19. *Head v. Timken Roller Bearing Company*, 486 F.2d 870 (1973).

20. "AT&T Settles with Government on Second Discrimination Suit," *Women Today*, 4 (June 10, 1974), p. 72. This is not the same action involving AT&T reported earlier in Chapter 1 in which AT&T agreed to pay $2.5 million to correct deficiencies uncovered in the affirmative action consent decree outlined earlier.

21. *Women Today*, 4 (April 29, 1974), p. 53.

22. Betty Richardson, *Sexism in Higher Education* (New York: The Seabury Press, 1974), p. 179.

23. Davidson, Ginsburg, and Kay, *Sex-based Discrimination*, p. 578.

24. *Contractors Association of Eastern Pennsylvania* v. *Secretary of Labor* 442 F.2d 159, cert. denied 404 U.S. 854, 92 S.Ct. 98, 30 L.Ed.2d 95 (1971).

25. "Sex Bias Hearings: Move to Halt U.S. Funds for University of Texas."

26. Revised Order Number 4, Section 60, subpart A, 2.1 paragraph (c), point 1, as reprinted in *Affirmative Action and Equal Employment: A Guidebook for Employers*. Relevant portions of Revised Order Number 4 are contained in Appendix A.

27. Ibid.

28. Revised Order Number 4, Section 60, subpart B, 2.11, paragraph (a).

29. Ibid., point 2.

30. Revised Order Number 4, Section 60, subpart B, 2.12, paragraph (e).

31. Revised Order Number 4, Section 60, subpart B, 2.14.

32. Revised Order Number 4, Section 60, subpart B, paragraph (k) point 1.

33. Revised Order Number 4, Section 60, subpart C, 2.23.

34. Equal Employment Opportunity Commission Sex Discrimination Guidelines, Section 1604.2, paragraph (1), point (i), as reprinted in *Affirmative Action and Equal Employment: A Guidebook for Employers*. Relevant portions of the EEOC Sex Discrimination Guidelines are reprinted in Appendix A.

35. "Federal Agency Rulings," *The United States Law Week*, 43 (June 10, 1975), p. 2512. See also "HEW Regulations," *Federal Register*, 40 (May 4, 1975), p. 24127. Relevant portions of the Title IX regulations are reprinted in Appendix A.

36. Judicial decisions will not be long in coming, however. Brigham Young University has challenged several portions of Title IX regulations in a court suit brought in October 1975. Brigham Young University charged that some Title IX regulations ". . . prohibit or interfere with the teaching or practice of high moral principles." ["Brigham Young University Challenges Parts of Bias Law," *Chronicle of Higher Education* (October 28, 1975), pp. 1, 10, at p. 1.] The university specifically repudiated sections of Title IX regulations that would nullify its dress code and forbid it from requesting information from individuals concerning their marital status and possible pregnancies or abortions.

37. John T. Dunlop, as reported in Cheryl M. Fields, "Affirmative Action: Changes in the Offing?" *Chronicle of Higher Education* (August 18, 1975), p. 3.

38. Ibid.

39. Carnegie Council on Policy Studies in Higher Education, *Making Affirmative Action Work* (forthcoming, Jossey-Bass, Inc., San Francisco), as previewed and reported in "Affirmative Action: Changes in the Offing?" p. 3, and "Carnegie Council's Affirmative Action Recommendations," *Chronicle of Higher Education* (August 18, 1975), pp. 3-4.

40. Peter E. Holmes, as reported in "HEW Statement Could Mark an End to Affirmative Action as It Has Been Known," *Women Today*, 5 (January 6, 1975), p. 1.

41. Ibid.

42. "Affirmative Action: Changes in Offing?", p. 3.

43. Ibid.

44. Ibid.

45. *Women Today*, 4 (December 23, 1974), p. 165.

46. Ibid.

47. Ibid.

48. Theodore Caplow, *The Academic Marketplace* (New York: Basic Books, 1958).

49. Richardson, *Sexism in Higher Education,* pp. 92-99.

50. See, in addition to Richardson, Judith Stacey, Susan Bereaud, and Joan Daniels (ed.), *And Jill Came Tumbling after: Sexism in American Education* (New York: Dell Books, 1974); also, Nancy Frazier and Myrna Sadker, *Sexism in School and Society* (New York: Harper and Row, 1973).

51. *Women Today*, 5 (May 26, 1975), p. 63.

Chapter 3
Theories of Sex Discrimination

1. Gary S. Becker, *The Economics of Discrimination*, 2d ed., (Chicago: University of Chicago Press, 1971).

2. Ibid. Very few new developments in economic theory are produced without one or more strokes in that direction by preceding economists. In the case of Becker's neoclassical theory, several writers including F.Y. Edgeworth seem to have hinted at a Becker type of analysis. For a pedagogical note on this matter, see Ray Marshall, "The Economics of Racial Discrimination: A Survey," *Journal of Economic Literature*, 12 (September 1974), pp. 849-871.

3. See, for example, Janet F. Madden, *The Economics of Sex Discrimination* (Lexington, Mass.: Lexington Books, 1973), chapter 4.

4. Becker, *The Economics of Discrimination*, p. 14.

5. Ibid., p. 14.

6. Ibid., p. 14.

7. Madden, *The Economics of Sex Discrimination*, p. 47.

8. Kenneth J. Arrow, "The Theory of Discrimination," in Orley Ashenfelter and Albert Rees (eds.), *Discrimination in Labor Markets* (Princeton, N.J.: Princeton University Press, 1974). See also Arrow's earlier, "Models of Job Discrimination" and "Some Models of Race in the Labor Market," in A.H.

Pascal (ed.), *Racial Discrimination in Economic Life* (Lexington, Mass.: Lexington Books, 1972).

9. Madden also identifies eight assumptions upon which the Becker model of discrimination is based. Madden, however, develops a variant of the model in which the input supply curves of the male and female societies are infinitely *inelastic* with respect to wages. This results, as we shall shortly see, in the conclusion that the male society gains from discrimination rather than losing. See Madden, *The Economics of Sex Discrimination,* pp. 45-46.

10. This is an implication of the Hecksher-Ohlin theorem of international trade. See especially Eli Hechsher, "The Effect of Foreign Trade on the Distribution of Income," *Ekonomisk Tidskrift,* 21 (1919), pp. 497-512.

11. The factor price equalization theorem, according to Takayama, ". . . asserts that the relative and absolute prices of the factors of production will eventually be equalized between the countries." Akira Takayama, *International Trade* (New York: Holt, Rinehart, and Winston, Inc., 1972), p. 88. The theorem was originally demonstrated by Eli Hecksher in "The Effect of Foreign Trade on the Distribution of Income" (see note 10), but was popularized by Paul Samuelson in "International Trade and the Equalization of Factor Prices," *Economic Journal,* 58 (June 1948), pp. 163-184.

12. See Madden, *The Economics of Sex Discrimination*, pp. 49-50 and 107-109.

13. Joan Robinson, *The Economics of Imperfect Competition* (London: MacMillan and Company, Ltd., 1965).

14. Martin Bronfenbrenner, "Potential Monopsony in Labor Markets," *Industrial and Labor Relations Review*, 9 (April 1956), pp. 577-588.

15. Lester C. Thurow, *Poverty and Discrimination* (Washington, D.C.: The Brookings Institution, 1969), especially chapter 7.

16. Madden, *The Economics of Sex Discrimination.*

17. This is a standard result which may be confirmed in James V. Koch, *Microeconomic Theory and Applications* (Boston: Little, Brown, and Company, 1976), p. 337.

18. It is not clear from empirical evidence either that $\theta_F < \theta_M$ in the entire economy. It may be true, however, that in specific occupations $\theta_F < \theta_M$. See, for example, Jacob Mincer, "Labor Force Participation of Married Women: A Study of Labor Supply," in *Aspects of Labor Economics* (Princeton: Princeton University Press, 1962); and Glen Cain, *Married Women in the Labor Force* (Chicago: University of Chicago Press, 1966).

19. The first public discussion of the overcrowding hypothesis was undertaken by Millicent Fawcett, "Equal Pay for Equal Work," *Economic Journal,* 28 (March 1918), pp. 1-6. See subsequent discussion by F.Y. Edgeworth, "Equal Pay to Men and Women for Equal Work," *Economic*

Journal, 32 (December 1922), pp. 431–457; and Robinson, *The Economics of Imperfect Competition,* pp. 301–304.

20. Valerie K. Oppenheimer, *The Female Labor Force in the United States* (Berkeley, Calif.: University of California Monograph Series, No. 5, 1970).

21. Barbara R. Bergmann, "The Effect on White Incomes of Discrimination in Employment," *Journal of Political Economy,* 79 (March–April, 1971), pp. 294–313.

22. Ibid., p. 303.

23. Karl Marx, *Capital, A Critique of Political Economy,* Vols. 1, 2, 3 (New York: Random House, 1906).

24. Frederick Engels, *The Origin of the Family, Private Property, and the State* (New York: International Publishers, 1942).

25. August Bebel, *Woman and Socialism* (New York: International Publishers, 1938).

Chapter 4
A Review of Empirical Studies of Sex Discrimination
and Affirmative Action

1. Barbara R. Bergmann and Myles Maxfield, "How to Analyze the Fairness of Faculty Women's Salaries on Your Own Campus," *AAUP Bulletin,* 61 (October 1975), pp. 262–265.

2. Ibid., p. 264.

3. "NCES Statistics Show Gap between Men and Women Faculty Continues," *Women Today,* 5 (March 3, 1975), p. 29.

4. Henry Sanborn, "Pay Differences between Men and Women," *Industrial and Labor Relations Review,* 17 (July 1964), pp. 534–550.

5. Isabel V. Sawhill, "The Economics of Discrimination against Women: Some New Findings," *Journal of Human Resources,* 8 (Summer 1973), pp. 383–396.

6. James N. Morgan, Wilbur J. Cohen, Martin H. David, and Harvey E. Brazer, *Income and Welfare in the United States* (New York: McGraw-Hill Book Company, 1962).

7. Victor Fuchs, "Differences in Hourly Earnings between Men and Women," *Monthly Labor Review,* 94 (May 1971), pp. 9–15.

8. Malcolm S. Cohen, "Sex Differences in Compensation," *Journal of Human Resources,* 6 (Fall 1971), pp. 434–447.

9. Ronald Oaxaca, "Male-Female Wage Differentials in Urban Labor Markets," *International Economic Review,* 14 (October 1973), pp. 673–709.

10. Larry E. Suter and Herman P. Miller, "Components of Income Differences between Men and Women," *Journal of Sociology* (forthcoming).

11. Richard B. Mancke, "Lower Pay for Women: A Case of Economic Discrimination?" *Industrial Relations*, 10 (October 1971), pp. 316-326.

12. For example, the most recent salary survey was published in the *AAUP Bulletin*, 61 (Summer 1975), pp. 118-199.

13. Alan E. Bayer and Helen S. Astin, "Sex Differentials in the Academic Reward System: What Changes Have There Been Since the Implementation of Federal Antibias Regulations?" *Science*, 198 (May 28, 1975), pp. 796-802.

14. Ibid., p. 801.

15. Ibid.

16. Helen S. Astin, *The Woman Doctorate in America: Origins, Career, and Family* (New York: Russell Sage Foundation, 1969).

17. Bayer and Astin, "Sex Differentials in the Reward System," p. 798.

18. Ibid.

19. Ibid., p. 799.

20. Ibid.

21. Ibid.

22. Alan M. Cartter and Wayne E. Ruhter, *The Disappearance of Sex Discrimination in First Job Placements of New Ph.D.'s* (Los Angeles: Higher Education Research Institute, 1975).

23. Bayer and Astin, "Sex Differentials in the Reward System," p. 800.

24. Ibid.

25. Ibid.

26. John J. Siegfried and Kenneth J. White, "Teaching and Publishing as Determinants of Academic Salaries," *Journal of Economic Education,* 4 (Spring 1973), pp. 90-99; see also their "Financial Rewards to Research and Teaching: A Case Study of Academic Economists," *American Economic Review,* 63 (May 1973), pp. 309-315.

27. David A. Katz, "Faculty Salaries, Promotions, and Productivity at a Large University," *American Economic Review,* 63 (June 1973), pp. 469-477.

28. Ibid., p. 474. The scholarly productivity index was based upon the partial regression coefficients estimated in Equation (4.2). A published book was assigned a weight of 230 points, while an excellent journal article was valued at 102 points.

29. Ibid., p. 477.

30. The concept of specific human capital is used by George E. Johnson and Frank P. Stafford, "The Earnings and Promotion of Women Faculty," *American Economic Review,* 64 (December 1974), pp. 888-903. The term was originally coined by Elisabeth Landes in "Male-Female Differences in Wages and Employment: A Specific Human Capital Model," unpublished doctoral dissertation, Columbia University, 1974.

31. Landes, p. 22.

32. James V. Koch and John F. Chizmar, "The Influence of Teaching and Other

Factors upon Absolute Salaries and Salary Increments at Illinois State University," *Journal of Economic Education*, 5 (Fall 1973), pp. 27-34.

33. Marianne A. Ferber, "Professors, Performance, and Rewards," *Industrial Relations*, 13 (February 1974), pp. 69-77.

34. Barbara B. Reagan and Betty J. Maynard, "Sex Discrimination in Universities: An Approach through Internal Labor Market Analysis," *AAUP Bulletin*, 60 (March 1974), pp. 13-21.

35. Ibid., p. 18.

36. Ibid.

37. Ibid., p. 14.

38. George E. Johnson and Frank P. Stafford, "The Earnings and Promotion of Women Faculty," *American Economic Review*, 64 (December 1974), pp. 888-903.

39. Yoram Ben-Porath, "The Production of Human Capital and the Life Cycle of Earnings," *Journal of Political Economy*, 75 (August 1967), pp. 352-365.

40. Sherwin Rosen, "Learning and Experience in the Labor Market," *Journal of Human Resources*, 7 (Summer 1972), pp. 326-342.

41. Johnson and Stafford extrapolated from the 1970 United States Census the information that the typical male academic worked 1,760 hours per year, while the comparable figure for female academics was only 1,200 hours per year. Johnson and Stafford, "The Earnings and Promotion of Women Faculty," p. 892.

42. In a related vein, Rosen has argued that prestigious institutions do not need to pay their novice faculty as much as less prestigious institutions because the prestigious institutions typically offer nonmonetary benefits and on-the-job training to new assistant professors. Rosen, "Earning and Experience in the Labor Market."

43. Johnson and Stafford, "The Earnings and Promotion of Women Faculty," from Table 3, p. 894.

44. Astin, *The Woman Doctorate in America: Origins, Career, and Training.*

45. Johnson and Stafford, "The Earnings and Promotion of Women Faculty," p. 901.

46. Ibid., p. 902.

47. *Board of Regents of the University of Nebraska* v. *A. Neil Dawes*, United States Court of Appeals, Eighth Circuit, No. 75-1126, August 26, 1975.

48. James V. Koch and John F. Chizmar, Jr., "Sex Discrimination and Affirmative Action in Faculty Salaries," *Economic Inquiry* (forthcoming, March 1976).

49. Tsuchigane and Dodge, *Economic Discrimination against Women in the United States*, p. 36.

50. Johnson and Stafford, "The Earnings and Promotion of Women Faculty," p. 892.

51. Ibid., p. 891.
52. Tsuchigane and Dodge, *Economic Discrimination against Women in the United States*, p. 40.
53. Robert Tsuchigane and Norton Dodge report that in the year 1960 the American Management Association regarded the net cost of a typical "quit" as $500. Ibid., p. 41.
54. "Labor Turnover of Women Factory Workers, 1950–1955," *Monthly Labor Review*, 78 (August 1955), pp. 889–894.
55. Edward J. O'Boyle, "Job Tenure: How It Relates to Race and Job," *Monthly Labor Review*, 92 (September 1969), pp. 16–23.
56. See, for example, Paula A. Armknecht and John Early, "Quits in Manufacturing: A Study of Their Causes," *Monthly Labor Review*, 95 (November 1972), pp. 31–37; also, the same authors' "Manufacturing Quit Rates Revisited," *Monthly Labor Review*, 96 (November 1973), pp. 53–56; and Vladimir Stoikov and R.L. Raimon, "Determinants of Differences in the Quit Rate among Industries," *American Economic Review*, 58 (December 1968), pp. 1283–1298.
57. Tsuchigane and Dodge, *Economic Discrimination against Women in the United States*, Table 4-1, p. 32.
58. Astin, *The Woman Doctorate in America: Origins, Career, and Training*.
59. See, for example, Richard M. Levinson, "Sex Discrimination and Employment Practices: An Experiment with Unconventional Job Inquiries," *Social Problems*, 22 (April 1975), pp. 533–543. An extensive bibliography accompanies this article.

Chapter 5
The Empirical Work

1. Bayer and Astin, "Sex Differentials in the Reward System."
2. John E. Caffrey, "Starting Salaries by Field," American Council on Education, 1968.
3. Bergmann and Maxfield take this position. See Bergmann and Maxfield, "how to Analyze the Fairness of Faculty Women's Salaries on Your Own Campus."
4. John F. Chizmar, "The Determination of Academic Rank at Illinois State University," unpublished report.
5. Johnson and Stafford, "The Earnings and Promotion of Women Faculty."
6. Ibid.
7. *Regents* v. *Dawes* (1975).
8. Ben-Porath, "The Production of Human Capital and the Life Cycle of Earnings."
9. Zvi Griliches, "Hedonic Price Indexes for Automobiles: An Econometric Analysis of Quality Change," *Government Price Statistics*, U.S. Congress,

Joint Economic Committee (Washington, D.C.: U.S. Government Printing Office, 1961), pp. 173-196.

10. Johnson and Stafford, "The Earnings and Promotion of Women Faculty."

11. Ibid., p. 893.

12. Donald E. Farrar and R.R. Glauber, "Multicollinearity in Regression Analysis: The Problem Revisited," *Review of Economic and Statistics*, 49 (February 1967), pp. 92-107.

Bibliography

AAUP Bulletin, 61 (Summer 1975): 118-199.

Armknecht, Paula A., and Early, John. "Manufacturing Quit Rates Revisited," *Monthly Labor Review*, 96 (November 1973): 53-56.

____ and ____ . "Quits in Manufacturing: A Study of Their Causes," *Monthly Labor Review*, 95 (November 1972): 31-37.

Arrow, Kenneth J. "Models of Job Discrimination," and "Some Models of Race in the Labor Market," in A.H. Pascal (ed.) *Racial Discrimination in Economic Life*. Lexington, Mass.: Lexington Books, 1972.

____ "The Theory of Discrimination," in Orley Ashenfelter and Albert Rees (eds.), *Discrimination in Labor Markets*. Princeton: Princeton University Press, 1974.

Astin, Helen S. *The Woman Doctorate in America: Origins, Career, and Family*. New York: Russel Sage Foundation, 1969.

"AT&T Agrees to Pay $2.5 Million to Correct EEO Settlement Deficiencies," *Women Today*, 5 (May 26, 1975): 64.

AT&T Settles with Government on Second Discrimination Suit," *Women Today*, 4 (June 10, 1974): 72.

Bayer, Alan E., and Astin, Helen S. "Sex Differentials in the Academic Reward System: What Changes Have There Been Since the Implementation of Federal Antibias Regulations?" *Science*, 198 (May 28, 1975): 796-802.

Bebel, August. *Women and Socialism*. New York: International Publishers, 1942.

Becker, Gary S. *The Economics of Discrimination*. Chicago: University of Chicago Press, 1957.

____ *The Economics of Discrimination*, 2d ed. Chicago: University of Chicago Press, 1971.

Ben-Porath, Yoram, "The Prediction of Human Capital and the Life Cycle of Earnings," *Journal of Political Economy*, 75 (August 1967): 352-365.

Bergmann, Barbara R. "The Effect on White Incomes of Discrimination in Employment," *Journal of Political Economy*, 79 (March–April 1971): 294-313.

____ and Maxfield, Myles, Jr. "How to Analyze the Fairness of Faculty Women's Salaries on Your Own Campus," *AAUP Bulletin*, 61 (October 1975): 262-265.

Brewster, Kingman, as quoted in Scully, Malcolm G. "Private Colleges Urged to

149

Establish Own Lobby," *The Chronicle of Higher Education*, (January 26, 1976): 3.

"Brigham Young University Challenges Parts of Bias Law," *Chronicle of Higher Education*, (October 28, 1975): 1, 10, at p. 1.

Bronfenbrenner, Martin. "Potential Monopsony in Labor Markets," *Industrial and Labor Relations Review*, 9 (April 1956): 577-588.

Caffrey, John E. "Starting Salaries by Field." American Council on Education, 1968.

Cain, Glen. *Married Women in the Labor Force.* Chicago: University of Chicago Press, 1966.

Caplow, Theodore. *The Academic Marketplace.* New York: Basic Books, 1958.

Carnegie Council on Policy Studies in Higher Education. *Making Affirmative Action Work*, as reported in "Affirmative Action: Changes in the Offing?" and "Carnegie Council's Affirmative Action Recommendations." *Chronicle of Higher Education*, (August 18, 1975).

Chizmar, John F., Jr. "The Determination of Academic Rank at Illinois State University," unpublished report.

Cohen, Malcolm S. "Sex Differences in Compensation," *Journal of Human Resources*, 6 (Fall 1971): 434-447.

Davidson, Kenneth M., Ginsburg, Ruth B., and Kay, Herma H. *Sex-based Discrimination: Text, Cases, and Materials.* St. Paul: West Publishing Company, 1974.

de Tocqueville, Alexis. *Democracy in America*, in Part 2, Reeves Translation (1840), in *World's Classics Series.* New York: Galaxy Books, 1947: 400.

Dunlop, John T., as reported in Cheryl M. Fields. "Affirmative Action: Changes in the Offing?" *Chronicle of Higher Education*, (August 18, 1975): 3.

Edgeworth, F.Y. "Equal Pay to Men and Women for Equal Work," *Economic Journal*, 32 (December 1922): 431-457.

Engels, Frederick. *The Origin of the Family, Private Property, and the State.* New York: International Publishers, 1942.

Farrar, Donald E. and Glauber, R.R. "Multicollinearity in Regression Analysis: The Problem Revisited," *Review of Economics and Statistics*, 49 (February 1967): 92-107.

Fawcett, Millicent. "Equal Pay for Equal Work." *Economic Journal*, 28 (March 1918): 1-6.

"Federal Agency Rulings." *The United States Law Week*, 43 (June 10, 1975): 2512.

Ferber, Marianne A. "Professors, Performance, and Rewards," *Industrial Relations*, 13 (February 1974): 69-77.

Frazier, Nancy, and Sadker, Myrna. *Sexism in School and Society.* New York: Dell Books, 1974.

Freund, Paul A., Sutherland, Arthur E., Howe, Mark D., and Brown, Ernest J. *Constitutional Law: Cases and Other Problems* Vol. 1. Boston: Little, Brown and Company, 1961.

Friedman, Milton. "The Methodology of Positive Economics," *Essays in Positive Economics*. Chicago: University of Chicago Press, 1953: 3-43.

Fuchs, Victor. "Differences in Hourly Earnings between Men and Women," *Monthly Labor Review*, 94 (May 1971): 9-15.

"Government's First Complaint: University of Maryland Charged with Bias," *Chronicle of Higher Education*, (October 28, 1975): 10.

Griliches, Zvi. "Hedonic Price Indexes for Automobiles: An Econometric Analysis of Quality Change," *Government Price Statistics*, U.S. Congress, Joint Economic Committee. Washington, D.C.: U.S. Government Printing Office, 1961: 173-196.

Gruberg, Martin. *Women in American Politics*. Oshkosh, Wis.: Academic Press, 1968: 4.

Hecksher, Eli. "The Effect of Foreign Trade on the Distribution of Income," *Ekonomisk Tidskrift*, 21 (1919): 497-512.

"HEW Regulations," *Federal Register*, 40 (May 4, 1975).

Holmes, Peter E., as reported in "HEW Statement Could Mark an End to Affirmative Action as It Has Been Known," *Women Today*, 5 (January 6, 1975): 1.

Johnson, George E., and Stafford, Frank D. "The Earnings and Promotion of Women Faculty," *American Economic Review*, 64 (December 1974): 888-903.

Johnson, Sheila K. "It Is Action, but Is It Affirmative?" *The New York Times Magazine*, (May 11, 1975): 18-33.

Johnston, John D., and Knapp, Charles L. "Sex Discrimination by Law: A Study in Judicial Perspective," *New York University Law Review*, 46 (October 1971): 676.

Katz, David A. "Faculty Salaries, Promotions, and Productivity at a Large University," *American Economic Review*, 63 (June 1973): 469-477.

Keynes, John N. *The Scope and Method of Political Economy*. London: Macmillan and Company, 1891.

Koch, James V. *Microeconomic Theory and Applications*. Boston: Little, Brown, and Company, 1976.

_____ and Chizmar, John F. "Sex Discrimination and Affirmative Action in Faculty Salaries," *Economic Inquiry*, (forthcoming, March, 1976).

_____ and _____. "The Influence of Teaching and Other Factors upon Absolute Salaries and Salary Increments at Illinois State University," *Journal of Economic Education*, 5 (Fall 1973): 27-34.

"Labor Turnover of Women Factory Workers, 1950-1955," *Monthly Labor Review*, 78 (August 1955): 889-894.

Landes, Elisabeth. "Male-Female Differences in Wages and Employment: A Specific Human Capital Model," unpublished doctoral dissertation. Columbia University, 1974.

Lepper, Mary M. "Affirmative Action Scored," *The Chronicle of Higher Education*, 8 (July 8, 1974): 8.

Lester, Richard A. *Antibias Regulations of Universities: Faculty Problems and Their Solutions.* New York: McGraw-Hill Book Company, 1974.

Levinson, Richard M. "Sex Discrimination and Employment Practices: An Experiment with Unconventional Job Inquiries," *Social Problems*, 22 (April 1975): 533-543.

Madden, Janet F. *The Economics of Sex Discrimination.* Lexington, Mass.: Lexington Books, 1973.

Mancke, Richard B. "Lower Pay for Women: A Case of Economic Discrimination?" *Industrial Relations*, 10 (October 1971): 316-326.

Marshall, Ray. "The Economics of Racial Discrimination: A Survey," *Journal of Economic Literature*, 12 (September 1974): 849-871.

Marx, Karl. *Capital, A Critique of Political Economy* Vols. 1, 2, 3. New York: Random House, 1906.

Mincer, Jacob. "Labor Force Participation of Married Women: A Study of Labor Supply," in *Aspects of Labor Economics.* Princeton: Princeton University Press, 1962.

Morgan, James N., Cohen, Wilbur J., David, Martin H., and Brazer, Harvey E. *Income and Welfare in the United States.* New York: McGraw-Hill Book Company, 1962.

Murphy, Thomas E. "Female Wage Discrimination: A Study of the Equal Pay Act, 1963-1970," *University of Cincinnati Law Review*, 39 (Fall 1970): 615-649.

"NCES Statistics Show Gap between Men and Women Faculty Continues," *Women Today*, 5 (March 3, 1975): 29.

New York Herald, as reported in Kraditor, Aileen S. *Up from the Pedestal: Selected Writings in the History of American Feminism.* Chicago: Quadrangle Books, 1968: 190.

Oaxaca, Ronald. "Male-Female Wage Differentials in Urban Labor Markets," *International Economic Review*, 14 (October 1973): 673-709.

O'Boyle, Edward J. "Job Tenure: How It Relates to Race and Job," *Monthly Labor Review*, 92 (September 1969): 16-23.

Okun, Arthur M. *Equality and Efficiency.* Washington, D.C.: The Brookings Institution, 1975.

Oppenheimer, Valerie K. *The Female Labor Force in the United States.* Berkeley, Calif.: University of California Monograph Series, No. 5, 1970.

Reagan, Barbara B., and Maynard, Betty J. "Sex Discrimination in Universities: An Approach through Internal Labor Market Analysis," *AAUP Bulletin*, 60 (March 1974): 13-21.

_____ and _____. "Sex Discrimination in Universities: An Approach through Internal Labor Market Analysis," *Bulletin of the American Association of University Professors*, 64 (June 1974): 419-427.

Richardson, Betty. *Sexism in Higher Education.* New York: The Seabury Press, 1974: 179.

Robinson, Joan. *The Economics of Imperfect Competition.* London: Mac-Millan and Company, Ltd., 1965.

Rosen, Sherwin. "Learning and Experience in the Labor Market," *Journal of Human Resources,* 7 (Summer 1972): 326-342.

Samuelson, Paul. "International Trade and the Equalization of Factor Prices," *Economic Journal,* 58 (June 1948): 163-184.

Sanborn, Henry. "Pay Differences between Men and Women," *Industrial and Labor Relations Review,* 17 (July 1964): 534-550.

Sawhill, Isabel V. "The Economics of Discrimination against Women: Some New Findings," *Journal of Human Resources,* 8 (Summer 1973): 383-396.

"Sex-Bias Hearings: Move to Halt U.S. Funds for University of Texas," *Chronicle of Higher Education,* (October 14, 1975): 12.

Siegfried, John J., and White, Kenneth J. "Financial Rewards to Research and Teaching: A Case Study of Academic Economists," *American Economic Review,* 63 (May 1973): 309-315.

_____ and _____. "Teaching and Publishing as Determinants of Academic Salaries," *Journal of Economic Education,* 4 (Spring 1973): 90-99.

Stacey, Judith, Bereaud, Susan, and Daniels, Joan (eds.) *And Jill Came Tumbling After: Sexism in American Education.* New York: Dell Books, 1974).

Stoikov, Vladimir, and Raimon, R.L. "Determinants of Differences in the Quit Rate among Industries," *American Economic Review,* 58 (December 1968): 1283-1298.

Stone, Irving. *Those Who Love: A Biographical Novel of Abigail and John Adams.* Garden City: Doubleday, 1965.

Suter, Larry E., and Miller, Herman P. "Components of Income Differences between Men and Women," *Journal of Sociology* (forthcoming).

Takayama, Akira. *International Trade.* New York: Holt, Rinehart, and Winston, Inc., 1972.

Thurow, Lester C. *Poverty and Discrimination.* Washington, D.C.: The Brookings Institution, 1969.

Tsuchigane, Robert, and Dodge, Norton. *Economic Discrimination against Women in the United States.* Lexington, Mass.: Lexington Books, 1974.

"29 Institutions Warned by HEW that U.S. May Withhold Contracts," *Chronicle of Higher Education,* (June 23, 1975): 1.

U.S. Government Printing Office. *Affirmative Action and Equal Employment: A Guidebook for Employers,* 1974.

U.S. Government Printing Office, Joint Economic Committee. *Economic Problems of Women.* 93d Congress, 1st Session, 1974.

Women Today, 4 (April 29, 1974): 53.

Women Today, 4 (December 23, 1974): 165.

Women Today, 5 (January 6, 1975): 1.

Judicial Cases

Contractors Association of Eastern Pennsylvania v. Secretary of Labor, 442 F.2d
    159 (1971).
Diaz v. Pan-American Airways, 442 F.2d 385 (1971).
Green v. Board of Regents, 474 F.2d 594 (1973).
Griggs v. Duke Power Company, 401 U.S. 424 (1971).
Head v. Timken Roller Bearing Company, 486 F.2d 870 (1973).
Phillips v. Martin Marietta Corporation, 400 U.S. (1971).
Reed v. Reed, 404 U.S. (1971).
Regents v. Dawes (1975).
Rosenfeld v. Southern Pacific Company, 444 F.2d (1971).
Schultz v. Wheaton Glass Company, 421 F.2d 259 (1970).
Sprogis v. United Airlines, Inc., 444 F.2d 1194 (1971).
University of Nebraska v. Neil Dawes, U.S. Court of Appeals, Eighth Circuit,
    75-1126 (1975).

Index: Subjects

155

Index: Names

157

About the Authors

James V. Koch is Professor of Economics and Chairman of the Department of Economics at Illinois State University. His Ph.D. degree is from Northwestern University. He has taught at California State University at Los Angeles, the University of Grenoble, France, and Brown University. He has published two other books and about thirty journal articles.

John F. Chizmar, Jr., is Assistant Professor of Economics at Illinois State University. His Ph.D. degree is from Boston College. He has published several journal articles in the area of human capital. He has attained a national reputation in the area of computer assisted instruction and has pioneered the introduction of computer assisted instruction into Economics classes.